The Man Who Founded California

M. N. L. Couve de Murville

ARCHBISHOP OF BIRMINGHAM, ENGLAND

THE MAN WHO FOUNDED CALIFORNIA

The Life of Blessed Junípero Serra

IGNATIUS PRESS   SAN FRANCISCO

Cover art: *Junípero Serra*
© Trustees, Santa Barbara Archives
Cover design by Roxanne Mei Lum
Maps drawn by Brenda Knapp

© 2000 Ignatius Press, San Francisco

ISBN 0–89870–751–x
Library of Congress catalogue number 99–75406
Printed in Hong Kong by C & C Offset Printing Co., Ltd.

CONTENTS

ACKNOWLEDGEMENTS

I would like to thank His Eminence Cardinal Roger Mahony, Archbishop of Los Angeles. Through him I visited Mission San Fernando Rey in 1992, where I heard about Junípero Serra for the first time. Mgr. Francis Weber, Rector of the Mission and Archivist of the Diocese of Los Angeles, has maintained my interest in the subject over the ensuing years; I am most grateful to him for his hospitality and for sharing his expertise with me. I wish to thank many American friends for taking me to the sites and along the routes connected with the early Spanish settlers of California, especially Archbishop William J. Levada of San Francisco, Professor B. Doyce Nunis, Jr., Fr. Thomas Merson, Mr. Louis Stafford and his wife, Anita, and Mr. Steven Griswold. Thanks are due to Mother Francisca, O.C.D., Prioress of the Carmelite Monastery in Carmel, California, who kindly made available documentation of the cure attributed to Fr. Junípero Serra and examined by the Congregation for the Causes of Saints in 1986.

His Excellency Mgr. Teodoro Úbeda, Bishop of Palma, gave me invaluable help through his hospitality during my stay in Majorca. Thanks to him, I was put in touch with Dr. Bartomeu Font Obrador, who piloted my research in the public and private libraries in Palma; I learned a lot from him through conversation and on visits to Juniperan sites on the island. I would like to record my special indebtedness to this learned devotee of Blessed Junípero.

Many librarians have earned my sincere gratitude by their help in obtaining material I needed. I would like to mention especially

Fr. Virgilio Biasiol, O.F.M., Director of the Santa Barbara Mission Archive Library, California; Mr. John Atkinson, Librarian of the Franciscan Central Library at Canterbury; Mr. Simon Lawson of the Bodleian Library at Oxford; and Mr. Joe Garity of the Gleeson Library of the University of San Francisco. The Trustees of the Academy of American Franciscan History are to be thanked for their permission to quote extensively from their copyright publications.

As regards the medical aspects of this study, I have been guided by my brother, Dr. J. C. Couve de Murville, and by Dr. Patricia Crosby of Nuneaton. I am very grateful to them both. Mrs. Jennifer Davies is to be thanked for typing the numerous drafts of this book and for remaining undeterred by my handwritten emendations.

The following have read the text in draft and have made useful suggestions for its improvement: Mgr. Francis Weber, Professor Jocelyn Hillgarth, Fr. Andrew Beer, Fr. David McLoughlin, Fr. Robert Le Tellier, Fr. Paul Dean and Mr. Louis Stafford. I express my thanks to them while retaining full responsibility for any inaccuracies in the text and for the judgements I have expressed therein.

EXPLANATORY NOTES

Indians: The natives of California were called Indians by the Spaniards. This name was given to all the inhabitants of South and North America because Christopher Columbus, in sailing west across the Atlantic, was hoping to reach India; not realising that there was another continent in the way, he called the people he found there Indians. In more recent times, the descendants of the original populations of North America have come to object to being called Indians and, even more, to the term Red Indians. Preference has been expressed for such terms as Native Americans or Amerindians. I have normally used the term natives in this study to describe the populations that the Spaniards found in California. Fr. Junípero Serra also referred to the natives of California as *gentiles* and used the term *gentilidad* to describe their civilisation. For these I have used pagans or paganism, while keeping gentiles in the translations of the Academy of the American Franciscan History from which quotations are made.

Accentuation: *Junípero* is spelled thus in Spanish, indicating the stress on the second syllable.

The Californias: I use the term Lower California, *Baja California*, for the long peninsula in Mexico first called California by the Spaniards, and I use the term California for the present-day state of the United States of America that the Spaniards called *Alta California* (Upper California).

MAJORCA

MAJORCA

In the Capitol at Washington, D.C., there is a hall filled with greater than life-size statues of the pioneers who established the United States of America. It comes as a surprise to find among them the statue of a Franciscan friar.[1] He was chosen by California to be one of the two people each state was allowed to nominate for this honour. This friar, Junípero Serra, is known as the founder of California. He was beatified by Pope John Paul II in 1988, and his memory is kept alive by the missions he established in the eighteenth century between San Diego and San Francisco, on the western coast of the United States. The names of these missions evoke the inhabitants of the Court of Heaven, names like Santa Barbara, San Jose, Santa Clara and San Luis, in contrast to the Jacksons, Smithvilles and Yellow Snakes of more eastern states. Not only do the names survive; it is a delight to discover in California the remains of the missions that Junípero Serra founded, buildings now lovingly restored or rebuilt after years of neglect. In contrast to the concrete freeways, the skyscrapers and the holiday homes of the most populous state of the Union, with its thirty-six million inhabitants, these old Spanish missions have a charm all their own. The long arcaded cloisters, the fountains and olive trees of their courtyards, the dark churches with painted walls and golden altars, all these evoke the life of a departed age.

Mallorquin

Junípero Serra is known to us as a Spaniard, but to Spaniards he was a *Mallorquin*, that is, an inhabitant of Majorca, the largest of the

Balearic Isles off the Mediterranean coast of Spain. Majorca is a beautiful island; its beaches and its climate are so attractive that it is visited every year by more than seven million tourists, mostly from northern Europe. The capital is Palma, a walled city where the citadel of the former Moorish emirate overlooks the harbour next to the Gothic cathedral. In 1229 King James I of Aragon expelled the Moors, so Majorcans are conscious of being the product of the *reconquista*, the slow reconquest of Spain from Muslim domination that began in the early Middle Ages and ended with the capture of Granada in 1492.

But Majorcans are also conscious of belonging to a Mediterranean civilisation, with Moorish and Jewish antecedents and roots that go back farther still, to the time of the Roman settlements in the island. Their language, though Latin in origin, is different from Spanish and closer to Catalan and the *Occitan* of southern France. Majorcans are explorers and travellers, open to many cultures; it is significant that their best-known writer is Raymón Lull, a medieval mystic and visionary who sought common ground between Christianity, Judaism and Islam. Spaniards from the mainland, "the Peninsula", as Majorcans call it, sometimes consider the inhabitants of Majorca unreliable, but the difference between them is better expressed by the contrast in their styles of dancing. Spain is characterised by the staccato rhythm of Flamenco; in Palma, lilting melodies reminiscent of sea chanties accompany the lines and circles of dancers on the squares near the cathedral.

A range of limestone mountains, rising straight out of the sea on the north side of the island, shelters the fertile plain with its fields of melons, its vineyards and its groves of orange trees. Farmers in Majorca lived, not on isolated farms, but in villages, and in one of these, Petra, Junípero was born, the eldest son of Antonio Nadal Serra and Margarita Rosa Ferrer. He was baptised Miguel José on the day of his birth, 24 November 1713. His sister, Juana María, was born three years later, and there were three other children who died young. The Serras had a small farm, and their house still stands in the *Carrer des Barracar*, where a plaque records the birth of one of Majorca's most famous sons.

In Majorca there is only one bishop, at Palma, the capital. People took the opportunity of having their children confirmed whenever the bishop was on visitation in their parish, so Miguel was confirmed when he was not yet two years old. His first years were those of a child of the countryside; the conversation at home was of crops and of the care and breeding of cattle. As the seasons of the year came round, the whole family was out in the fields when help was needed, for planting and for bringing in the hay, for the olive harvest and the grape harvest. All this was to stand Junípero in good stead when the time came for him to introduce farming methods to the natives of the American continent.

On the hill above Petra, almost visible from his home, was the shrine of *Mare de Déu de Bon Any*, the Mother of God of the Good Year. Here the farmers came to pray, conscious as they were of the uncertainties of agricultural success. This devotion influenced Miguel's love of our Lady, and he was fond of coming back to this place. He was a small child, slightly built; although Antonio and Margarita Serra could not read or write, they wanted their son to have a better education, and so they took him to the school of the Franciscan Friary of San Bernadino at Petra, five minutes' walk from his home. There he learned the rudiments of reading and writing, mathematics and Latin; the friars taught him the truths of the Catholic religion, and they also taught him music, especially Gregorian chant. Miguel sang well and was a cantor at church services from time to time; but he was at hand to help with the work of the farm, especially during the long summer vacations, which coincided with harvest time.

PAGES 16–17   *The town of Petra, Majorca where Junípero Serra was born. On the left, the parish church of St. Peter. On the right, the Franciscan church of San Bernardino.*

Franciscan Vocation

When he was fifteen he told his parents that he wanted to be a priest. It was a sacrifice for a farming family to give up their only son in this way, but in September 1729 Antonio and Margarita took him to Palma and made an arrangement with one of the prebendaries of the cathedral, that is, a priest who worked at the cathedral and received his stipend, or *prebend*, from its revenues. In return for the payment of his board and lodgings at the priest's house, Miguel would learn how to recite the Divine Office in choir, and he would be under the tutorship of the priest, who would make sure that he attended lectures and kept reasonable hours. Miguel began his studies in scholastic philosophy at the Friary of St. Francis. This building still stands in the centre of the old city of Palma. Its double cloister, with delicate Gothic arcading, is one of the architectural gems of Majorca, and the great church of the friars contains the tomb of Raymón Lull. The friars taught their own students but also some diocesan seminarians and a few lay students, who were allowed to attend lectures as a privilege.

By the beginning of 1730, Miguel had decided that he wanted to become a Franciscan. He left the prebendary's home, ceased attending lectures and entered the novitiate. His parents did not have to pay for their son's board and lodging anymore, since he had embraced the life of one of the mendicant orders of the Catholic Church whose distinguishing mark was poverty. (The founder of the Franciscans had been known as the *Poverello*, the little poor man of Assisi, who gave up all his worldly possessions to be able to follow Christ more closely.) After six months, Miguel was considered sufficiently advanced to be clothed in the Franciscan habit; this took place on 14 September 1730. From then on he wore the grey tunic and hood, the white knotted cord and the sandals of the Greyfriars.

The house, number 6 Carrer de Barracar, Petra, Majorca, where Junípero Serra was born.

As a novice Miguel had to take part in all the menial tasks of the community. He also received his spiritual formation from the master of novices and learned about the history of the Franciscan Order, its Spanish provinces and their work on the missions. Although Miguel could read music, he was not much use when the friars came together to sing the Divine Office because he was too short to turn the pages of the Gradual, the huge parchment volume with plain-chant notation, which was placed on the lectern in the centre of the choir. The novice master decided that Miguel should serve the private Masses of the fathers instead; perhaps he was also mortifying a novice who was a little too conscious of having a beautiful voice.

On 15 September 1731, Miguel made his religious profession by pronouncing first vows as a Franciscan. Throughout his life he maintained a great devotion to that solemn promise by which he had committed himself to the service of Jesus Christ through a life of poverty, chastity and obedience, lived in the special service of the Holy See. Every year he renewed his vows on 16 April, the day when Pope Innocent III had given his approval to the Franciscan Rule in 1209. He would also renew them publicly whenever he was present at the profession of novices. As a sign of a person's commitment to become a new creation in Christ, religious profession was the occasion for taking a new name, and Miguel chose the name of one of St. Francis' companions known for his humility and simplicity, Brother Juniper. From then on, Miguel was known as Brother (*Fray* in Spanish) Junípero Serra. Junípero's family supported him in the choice he had made. In a letter written many years later, when he was on his way to America, he recalls words spoken to him by his father in support of his Franciscan vocation: "I well remember that, while assisting my father (I was already a religious at the time)

PAGE 20   *The font in St. Peter's church where Junípero Serra was baptised on November 24, 1713, the day of his birth*

PAGES 22–23   *Cloister of St. Francis' Friary, Palma, Majorca, where Junípero Serra studied and taught*

when he was taken so seriously ill that Extreme Unction became advisable—convinced he was to die and the two of us being alone—he said to me: 'Son, what I am most anxious about is that you be a good religious of our Father Saint Francis.' " [2]

The family farm went to Junipero's sister, Juana, and her husband, Miguel Ribot. The family continued to produce vocations. Junipero's nephew became a Capuchin; his great-nephew was a diocesan priest.

Student and Professor

It was now time for Fray Junipero to return to his studies. From 1731 to 1737 he studied, first, scholastic philosophy, then theology at St. Francis' Friary. But very soon he was appointed as philosophy lecturer at Saint Francis' and had to study much harder in order to prepare lectures. He was also writing his dissertation for a doctorate in theology. Meanwhile, he was ordained deacon on 17 March 1737. We do not know the date of his ordination to the priesthood, but it must have been in 1738 or 1739.

Junipero lectured on philosophy at St. Francis' Friary for six years, from 1737 to 1743. We have evidence of his philosophy teachings through the manuscript notes taken by one of his students, 404 pages neatly written and bound in vellum. This manuscript is now in the library of the Oratory of St. Philip in Palma. The notes cover logic and metaphysics; they consider the definition of substance and accidents, essence and being, the constitution of matter and the nature of the soul. They also include an account of the philosophy of Raymón Lull, but, although this was a hundred years after Descartes, there is no evidence of any desire to enter into dialogue with contemporary philosophy, no acknowledgement even of its existence.

In 1742 Junipero gained his doctorate in theology and was then appointed as professor of the Chair of Scotist Theology at the University of Palma. He was no longer teaching at St. Francis' Friary

Bible that Junípero Serra used as a student (now at the
College of La Sapienza, Palma, Majorca)

but at the Lullian University, as it was called. Junípero had tenure now and was teaching, not only Franciscan novices, but any students who signed up for his lectures in preparation for their degrees. There were nine lectureships in theology at the university. Junípero held the chair that gave its teaching according to the great Franciscan theologian of the Middle Ages, Blessed Duns Scotus (c. 1266–1308).

We do not have any precise indications about the theological teaching of Junípero while he was at the university, but it is likely to have been traditional, reproducing an ensemble of great sophistication as produced by the theological schools of northern Europe in the thirteenth century. However, by the time Serra started to teach theology, the eighteenth century was nearly halfway through its course, and the intellectual world had greatly altered since Scotus taught at Oxford, Paris and Cologne. The Protestant Reformation had removed half of Europe from the teaching authority of the Catholic Church; literary criticism was beginning to be applied to the Bible; the movement known as the Enlightenment was questioning the value of tradition in science and religion and urging that pure reason was the only criterion for the political activity of kings, politicians and social reformers. One wonders how far Junípero Serra prepared his students for the world they would encounter as adults.

Missionary

In 1749 Junípero Serra's life took an unexpected turn; he volunteered to go as a missionary to Mexico (*New Spain*, as it was then called) because of the appeals being made to Franciscans for help with this work. In explaining this step, Junípero spoke years later of the call that had led him to leave his native land: "I have had no other motive but to revive in my soul those intense longings which I have had since my novitiate when I read the lives of the saints. These longings had become deadened because of the preoccupation I had with studies."[3]

Junípero Serra felt the limitations of the static world of theology in eighteenth-century Spain. He had been in trouble with the Inquisition in 1739 and had been forbidden to teach two propositions that were probably connected with the Scotist doctrine of the Immaculate Conception of the Blessed Virgin Mary.[4] Did he suffer from the jealousies of academic life? There is a Majorcan proverb that says a lot: *Poble petit, llengua llarga*, "small village, long tongue". It could apply to academe, too. Anyway, in later life Junípero had come to see his studies as a distraction, and he considered that the lives of saints, especially of missionary martyrs, had first revealed to him his true calling: preaching the gospel to those who are ignorant of the Christian message. Whatever lesser motives may have prompted this decision, he now saw the missionary vocation as God's will for him.

Junípero was actually preaching a Lenten retreat at Petra when he received the news that he had been accepted for the missions, yet he did not tell his parents straightaway. He waited until he had reached Cádiz to send a letter, written in *Mallorquin*, to another friar, Fray Francesch Serra, asking him to read it to his parents. Perhaps he felt that if he broke the news to them himself, their distress would weaken his resolve. Certainly, his letter shows his deep affection and his sadness at the pain he is causing his family. He writes:

> Friend of my heart, on this occasion of my departure, words cannot express the feelings of affection that overwhelm me. I want to ask you again to do me the favor of consoling my parents, who, I know, are going through a great sorrow. . . . Tell them how badly I feel at not being able to stay longer and make them happy as I used to do. At any rate they know well that first things come first; and our first duty, undoubtedly, is to do the Will of God. Nothing else but the love of God has led me to leave them.[5]

With Junípero went another friar lecturer from Palma, Francisco Palóu, who was nine years younger and had been one of Junípero's students in the philosophy faculty. They volunteered separately and unknown to each other but were in fact together for most of

Junípero's time in California. Years later Palóu wrote the biography of his friend that is the main source for the early history of the missions in California.

> *As the coastline of Spain sank below the horizon, Junípero looked on Europe for the last time. He was in his thirty-sixth year, almost exactly halfway through his earthly course. . . .*

The Angry Ship's Captain

They set sail from Palma in an English vessel bound for Málaga. Palóu tells us about the English captain of the ship, who wanted to discuss doctrine with the two friars in broken Portuguese, convinced as he was that he could expose their religion as nonscriptural. He had seen all those statues of "idols" in Catholic churches and the disgraceful cult of the Virgin Mary. He had a soiled copy of the English Bible with him, so he must have read it regularly. Triumphantly he read out the text that he interpreted as utterly demolishing the arguments for Roman Catholicism. Junípero then read out another text, which went against the meaning the captain intended. The captain then tried to find another text and, when he failed, said grumpily that a page had been torn from his Bible. Then Junípero quoted something that went clearly in the Catholic sense: "There's something against that", said the captain, but again he could not find it in his Bible, which made him angry. He would not let the friars alone but brought up the matter of religion again and again. Once, when he was bested in the argument, he drew a dagger and put it at Junípero's throat; another time, he threw himself upon his bed in baffled fury, "[b]ut", comments Palóu, "the anger of that perverse heretic was restrained, and during the rest of the journey he was not so annoying as before."[6] Poor sea captain! There is nothing more infuriating than to be bested by an enemy whom one despises. Sadly, the captain typified English attitudes towards the Spaniards and their religion, attitudes that went on well into the nineteenth century. Charles Kingsley, in the popular story *Westward Ho!*, written in 1855, betrays the same prejudice as the irate captain with remarks like these: "These Spaniards are rank cowards, as all bullies are. They pray to a woman, the idolatrous rascals, and no wonder they fight like women."

At Málaga, the two friars found a ship bound for Cádiz, whence they sailed for America on 30 August 1749. As far as we know, it was Junípero's only visit to the Spanish mainland. As the coastline of Spain sank below the horizon, Junípero looked on Europe for the last time. He was in his thirty-sixth year, almost exactly halfway through his earthly course; the thirty-five years that remained to him were all spent in America, sixteen of them in what was to become his beloved California.

Thirst

Twenty Franciscans and seven Dominicans were on board, all bound for the missions. It took them seven weeks from Cádiz to Puerto Rico, the port of entry for the New World. Europeans had been sailing backwards and forwards across the Atlantic for more than two hundred and fifty years, but their voyages still had unexpected dangers and hardships. In this case the hardship came from the shortage of drinking water, which had been stored in leaking barrels. Junípero recalls, "The shortage of water was our greatest trial. I was so thirsty that I would not have hesitated to drink from the dirtiest puddle in the road or anything, no matter what."[7]

Undeterred by this trial during their voyage, the zealous Franciscans announced a mission as soon as they reached Puerto Rico because they were told that most of the population had not been to confession since the last mission, nine years previously. They scattered all over the city proclaiming a week of jubilee and summoning the people to a series of evening sermons at the cathedral. They heard confessions for most of the night afterwards. The whole of Puerto Rico came to hear the enthusiastic visitors from Spain, and the city council delayed their ship for a week, so eager were the inhabitants to hear the friars and benefit from their preaching and their counselling.

The next leg of the journey took the missionaries to Vera Cruz, on the coast of Mexico, but another hazard came from the wind, on which sailing ships were dependent; they were in sight of Vera Cruz when a fierce north wind blew them out to sea again. The ship was in poor condition, filling with water and threatening to lose its main mast, yet they had to spend several more days in a stormy sea before they could make land.

At last, on 7 December 1749, the missionaries disembarked on the mainland at Vera Cruz. It was 270 miles away from Mexico City, and horses were provided for the friars at the king of Spain's expense, but Fray Junípero and another friar obtained permission to walk the whole way. They were being faithful to the Rule of St. Francis, which forbade the friars to ride on horseback except in cases of real necessity, but it was also an indication of something absolute in Junípero's character. He wanted to offer the penance of a journey on foot so as to win the graces for the great endeavour he knew himself to be undertaking.

MEXICO

MEXICO

As Junípero and his companion followed the long road to the hinterland, they entered a colonial world, that is, one where the interest and profit of the colonial power were the first consideration of government. The most blatant example of this exploitation was the system for working the rich silver mines of Mexico, which produced a large percentage of the world's output. This bullion was shipped annually to Spain to prop up the economy of the mother country. The mines were worked by forced labour, native workers being compelled to move with their families to pitheads, sometimes hundreds of miles away. The working conditions were appalling; miners were kept underground in some cases for six consecutive working days and allowed to come up into daylight only on Sundays.

In colonial society, politics and religion were inextricably combined, because the coming of Spanish rule was identified with the extension of Christendom. The spread of the Catholic faith was specifically mentioned as the first aim of royal policy, but, in fact, the administration of the Church was firmly in the hands of the civil power by virtue of the *patronato real*, "the royal patronage". Ever since the early sixteenth century, the popes had granted the effective running of the Church in America to the kings of Spain. This meant that all appointments of bishops were made by the Crown and that every aspect of Church life was regulated by royal officials; nor were bishops allowed to report to Rome or to make regular visits to the pope, as Canon Law requires. Everything stopped at Madrid, and everything was decided in Madrid.

As the road rose steadily from sea level to an altitude of 7,500 feet, perhaps Junípero came to regret having spurned the King's horses. Palóu tells us what happened: "[W]ith fatigue the feet of the Venerable Father Junípero began to swell, so that when he arrived at a hacienda he could not stand. This swelling was attributed to mosquito bites because of the great itching he felt. Having rested there a day, unconsciously he rubbed the one leg too much while he was sleeping. In the morning it appeared all bloody so that a wound resulted which (as we shall see later) lasted during all his life."[1] The two friars arrived at the great shrine of Our Lady of Guadalupe on the outskirts of Mexico City on 31 December 1749, and the next day they reached the Missionary College of San Fernando, to which they had been assigned.

The College of San Fernando

Missionary colleges were a Franciscan contribution to the life of the Church, the first one having been founded in Rome in 1622 with a specialization in the Arab world. These colleges brought together selected members of the Order in a community trained for missionary work. They also acted as a haven to which missionaries could return after a time on the missions, when they needed to rest and to build up their strength, both spiritual and physical. The office of the Church, sung by the community, was an important part of the life of the college, because on the missions the fathers were isolated and not able to benefit from community prayer. The president of the college was the ecclesiastical superior of the missionaries, who reported to him regularly on their work. When the missionaries left one mission, they returned to the college until their next assignment. Old missionaries retired there and were looked after until they died. San Fernando was a large college with the second biggest church in Mexico City and room for a hundred friars. It had been founded in 1734 and already had a fine tradition. Fray Junípero was to belong to it until the end of his life and was obviously proud to do so.

When Fr. Junípero arrived at San Fernando, he was so full of enthusiasm that he asked to make his novitiate all over again; although this was not allowed by his superiors, he was authorised to join in with the prayers of the novices, after he had completed the round of prayer carried out by the community of professed friars.

The college required that new arrivals spend twelve months in residence, so as to have time to get used to life in America and also to become imbued with the spirit of the community. In the case of Junípero, this initial period lasted only five months, because a special opportunity in the Sierra Gorda Mission arose and the president of the college judged that Junípero could usefully take part. The Sierra Gorda is a mountainous and isolated region, 175 miles north of Mexico City. A certain number of *pueblos*, or towns, surrounded the region; these were inhabited by the descendants of Spanish settlers and Mexicans from other parts of the country; but in the mountains themselves only pagan natives lived, speaking their own language, Pame. The college of San Fernando had been asked to undertake missionary work there in 1744.

Junípero Serra and Francisco Palóu were assigned to the region, and once again they expressed their dedication to the Franciscan ideal by walking all the way; they arrived in June 1750. They found the mission system in full operation, so this proved to be a training ground for them in the methods they were to apply in California twenty years later.

Native Pueblos

The first characteristic of the Spanish missionary method had been formulated as early as 1519 by the Franciscan Juan de Quevedo, Bishop of Darien in Panama. He said that he tried to unite the Indians in *pueblos* and to keep them under constant supervision. The Franciscans in the Sierra Gorda had first of all selected good sites for farming, places with rich soil and plenty of water. Then they had built a chapel and invited the natives to come to live there and to

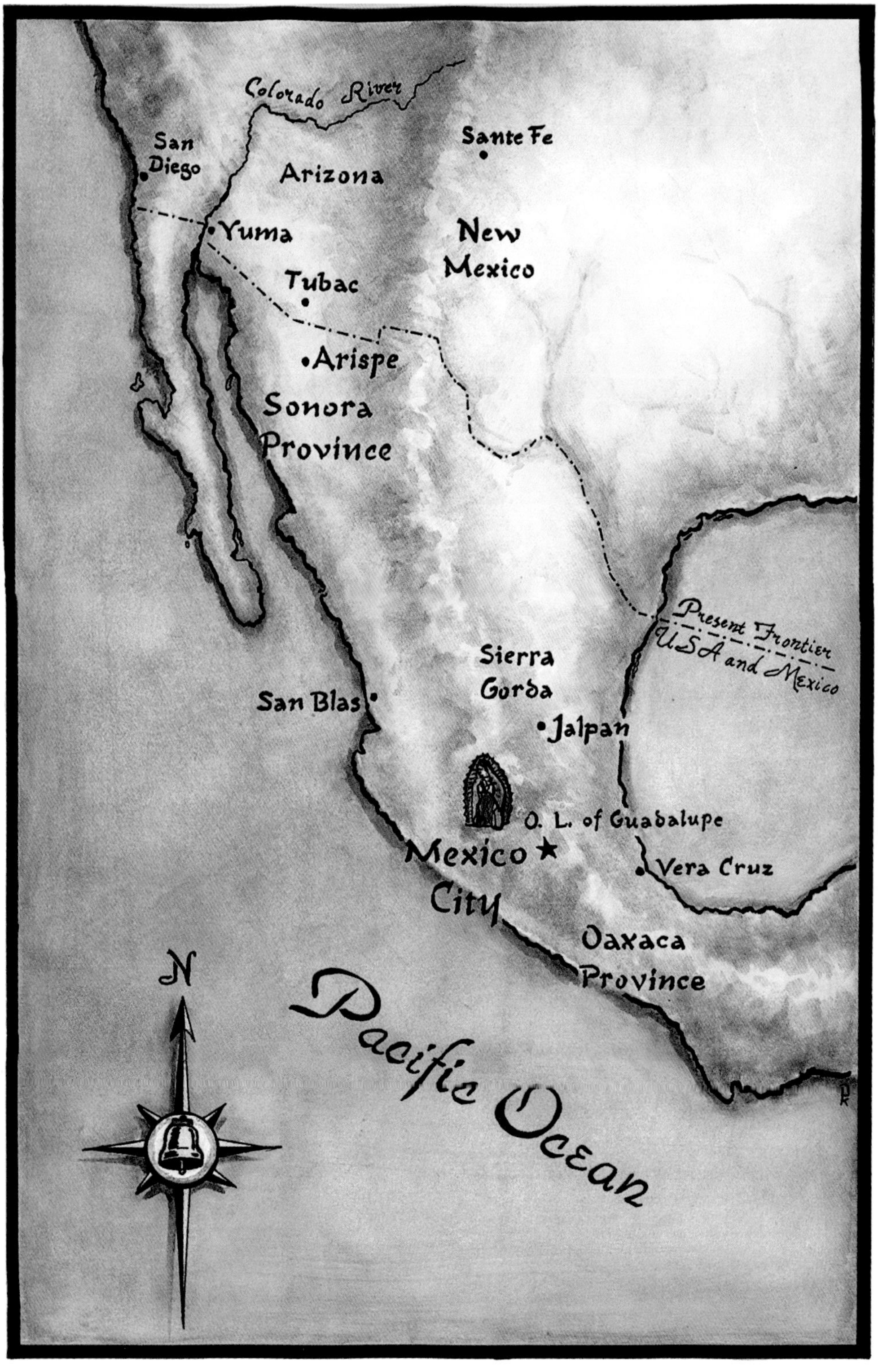

Colorado River
San Diego
Sante Fe
Arizona
Yuma
New Mexico
Tubac
Arispe
Sonora Province
Present Frontier U.S.A. and Mexico
Sierra Gorda
San Blas
Jalpan
O. L. of Guadalupe
Mexico City
Vera Cruz
Oaxaca Province
N
Pacific Ocean

become Christians. Once a native had been baptised he was considered a member of the Christian *pueblo* and under the authority of the missionaries. The mission became a large agricultural undertaking, with crops producing food for the natives, feeding hundreds and sometimes thousands of workers. In the Sierra Gorda the five missions thus established had brought together within two years 1,203 families, comprising more than four thousand individuals. A large number of trades were needed for such an enterprise, so the Indians were placed in apprenticeships. They learned agriculture, stock rearing, brick and tile making, pottery making, weaving, leather tanning, metalworking, brewing and cooking. Three times a day a bell would summon them from their fields and workshops, and this labour force would receive food distribution according to the needs of each family. Girls older than eleven, unmarried women and those whose husbands were not with them lived in a special building, the *monjerio*, which was kept locked at night.

Spanish law determined the second characteristic of the missionary method: the natives were considered to be spiritually and intellectually in the position of children. Since they could not yet be treated as adults, their freedom was severely restricted. They were free to refuse baptism, but, once they had been baptised, they were considered to be completely under the authority of the Franciscans. They could not leave the mission without permission; those who had misbehaved were punished. Since the missionaries were in the position of a father who was obliged to enforce discipline, corporal punishment was administered on occasion, just as it would have been given to children in those times.

According to the third principle applied by the missionaries, the mission, the land under cultivation and any money that the mission earned was destined to become eventually the property of the *pueblo*. Once the natives were ready to govern themselves and had become a truly Catholic community, the missionaries would leave and a diocesan priest would become the pastor. The new town would have the same status as any other *pueblo* of the Spanish colonial empire. There was no expropriation of land, as happened in many parts of North America. The system was paternalistic, but the purpose of the whole process was the good of the natives, as the missionaries saw it; that is, their Christianisation and their integration into Spanish society and culture.

Music and Drama

The friars noticed that the senses of sight and hearing were particularly developed among the natives, and so they made full use of these in the liturgy. Religious music was taught, both plainchant and polyphony. The friars also set religious words to Pame tunes. The great feasts of the Church were thus celebrated in a way that appealed particularly to the eye and to the ear. At Christmas young Pames would be taught to act out the events that accompanied the birth of Christ. Every Friday in Lent a procession went from the church to the top of the high hill nearby, and Junípero himself carried the cross while Palóu explained everything that had happened to Jesus at the fourteen "stations" on the way. On Palm Sunday there was another procession, with palm branches in everyone's hand, and the crowd sang and shouted its acclamation of Jesus, just as the inhabitants of Jerusalem had done when he came into their city.

On Maundy Thursday Junípero washed the feet of the twelve oldest men residing at the mission; then he ate a meal with them in front of a congregation. Afterwards he preached, explaining the meaning of what Jesus had done at the Last Supper. On Good Friday, the descent from the cross was reenacted. A life-size image of Christ, beautifully painted and with real hair, had been made in Mexico City, and this was attached to a cross. The limbs of the statue were articulated and hinged, so that it could be taken down from the cross in a realistic way and laid in a casket. Again, one of the friars preached and explained what had happened on the first Good Friday. In fact, the ceremonies of Holy Week were so well done at the mission that many of the Spaniards from the nearby *pueblos* would come to spend the week there year by year, making a sort of annual retreat.

Corpus Christi was another high spot of liturgical celebration. Junípero had a special devotion to this feast because it was like a royal progress of Christ through his own land. The consecrated Host was taken in procession through the whole settlement to the accompaniment of prayers and hymns. On the way, four chapels had been made of branches and rich cloth hangings. Each one had an altar on which was placed the monstrance, that is, the portable shrine made of silver gilt containing the Host. Then a young man would recite the praises of Christ in this wonderful Sacrament, in Spanish at two of the stations and in the Pame language at the other two.

Junípero realised the importance of having a fine church for his mission. It was designed, probably by an architect from Mexico City, in the spacious and much decorated style of Spanish baroque. It was made entirely of cut stone, and the building of it took seven years, because the labour was provided by the natives when they were not able to work in the fields. Junípero Serra and the other friars worked with them on the construction. Palóu records that Junípero was once working with a team of more than twenty men, transporting a heavy beam; because he was shorter than the others, he had to put a roll of cloth on his shoulder so that he could take the weight of the beam. The slight youth from Petra had grown into a short, stocky man. When Junípero's tomb at Carmel Mission, near Monterey, was opened in 1943, the anthropologists who examined the skeleton calculated that he had been five feet two inches in height.

PAGE 40   *The church of Jalpan in the mountainous region of the Sierra Gorda, Mexico.*

PAGE 41   *The interior of the church of Jalpan, Sierra Gorda, Mexico. Junípero Serra took part in the building of this church.*

The church at Jalpan is still there today, as are four other stone churches built by the Franciscans in the area; they are the parish churches of the *pueblos* that succeeded the missions.

Fray Junípero was in the Sierra Gorda for eight years. For three of these he was *padre presidente*, that is, the superior, of the other Franciscans, but he did not enjoy this very much and persuaded the authorities at San Fernando to let him become a simple missionary again. Then in 1758 he and Palóu were recalled to their college. For the next nine years, Serra remained at San Fernando, where he was successively choir master and master of novices. He was on the college council and he was a confessor, both inside the house and out. He was also one of the home missionaries, preaching in many different dioceses in various parts of the country.

Four Meanings of the Word "Mission"

"Home mission" is yet another use of that overused word *mission*, which has several different meanings. Mission is one of the basic words of Christianity, since it refers to the *sending* of someone to preach the gospel to those who have not yet heard it. It comes from the Latin word *mitto*, "I send", and thus translates the Greek word *apostello*, used in the New Testament. An *apostle* was someone who was sent by Jesus with a message of salvation, just as Jesus himself was sent by the Father to reconcile the world to God. Mission is thus a concept that is central to the work of the Church. In Catholic usage, mission describes, first, the sending of a missionary. Thus Serra received a mission to go to America to preach the gospel. Second, mission describes a community established by a missionary who has converted a certain number of the nonbelievers to whom he has been *sent*. "The mission" church is the place where that community gathers. Third, because of the particular methods used by the Franciscans in the Sierra Gorda and, later, in California, the "mission" came to mean an economic and agricultural enterprise under the control of the missionaries in order to create a Christian community that would later become a civil unit, the *pueblo*. In a way, the Franciscan missions in Mexico and California and the Jesuit missions in Paraguay (where they were called *reductions*) were like the monasteries of the Middle Ages in creating a large, autonomous, economic complex under ecclesiastical control, because of the dangers or inadequacies of the surrounding society.

Last, a "home mission" was the programme of spiritual renewal for an already established Christian community. Thus special preachers would come to a parish to "preach a mission" for a stated time, in order to renew the fervour of the faithful by a regular course of sermons, special services, opportunities for the Sacrament of Reconciliation and possibly visits to Catholics in their homes to rally the lapsed and put them in touch once again with the local church.

> *. . . the friars feared they would be devoured alive by insects if they kept out of the water and would be eaten by alligators if they fell in.*

While he was at San Fernando, Junípero travelled to many different parts of Mexico on these home missions, sometimes to remote areas like the province of Oaxaca in the mountainous south of the country, which could be reached only by uncharted tracks and perilous canoe journeys. The heat was excessive, and Palóu records that the friars feared they would be devoured alive by insects if they kept out of the water and would be eaten by alligators if they fell in. At night they dared not land because of the wild animals and snakes in the forest.

Palóu, in his life of Junípero, tells us a story of the friars on such a journey that plunges us straight into the atmosphere of the *Fioretti*, the early account of the life of St. Francis in which miraculous events seem to be part of everyday life. The Franciscans had been preaching in the area of the Huaxteco tribe, north of Jalpan.

When their apostolic labors were over, they returned to the college. One day during the journey, when the sun had already set, the missionaries did not know where to go for a night's lodging, believing for certain that they would have to spend the night in the open fields. They were thinking the matter over, when they saw a house a short distance away, close to the highway. They entered it to ask for shelter. Within they found a venerable man with his wife and a child, who graciously offered them shelter. With unusual neatness and kindness they also served them supper. After the fathers had said farewell next morning and had given thanks to their benefactors, they continued their journey. At a short distance they met some muleteers, who asked them where they had stayed overnight. The missionaries replied they stayed in the house near the road. "Which house?" queried the muleteers. "Along the entire road you traveled yesterday, there was not a house or a ranch for many leagues." The fathers stood looking at one another in wonderment, while the muleteers repeated their statement that there was no such house along the road. The missionaries then believed that it had been divine Providence which had granted them the favor of that hospitality, and that undoubtedly those persons who were within the house were Jesus, Mary and Joseph. They pondered not only on the neatness and cleanliness of the house, despite its poverty, and the affectionate tenderness with which they dispensed their hospitality, but also on the extraordinary inner consolation which they had felt in their hearts there. They gave God our Lord the thanks He deserved for the special favor they had received.[2]

A Lively Sermon

Junípero was also in demand for preaching missions in Mexico City. His biographer noted that "he tended to preach rather long sermons"; perhaps it was in order to make them more lively that he resorted once to a dramatic interlude to illustrate how dreadful sin is and how we should do penance. The interlude turned out to be more dramatic than he intended. Palóu describes it thus:

> During one of his sermons . . . he took out a chain, and after lowering his habit so as to uncover his back, having exhorted his hearers to penance, he began to scourge himself so violently that the entire congregation broke into tears. Thereupon, a man from the congre-

gation arose and hurriedly went to the pulpit, took the chain from the penitential Father, descended from the pulpit and went and stood in the highest part of the sanctuary. Imitating the venerable preacher, he uncovered himself to the waist and began to perform public penance, saying amid tears and sobs: "I am the sinner who is ungrateful to God, who ought to do penance for my many sins—and not the father, who is a saint." So violent and merciless were the strokes, that, before the whole congregation, he fell to the floor, they judging him dead. After he received the Last Sacraments where he fell, he died.[3]

Junípero obviously practised the emotional style of Franciscan preaching that aimed at speaking to the heart of the congregation and making them weep for their sins. Sometimes when in the pulpit he would produce a large stone; lifting up the crucifix in one hand, he would beat his breast with the stone so hard that the faithful were afraid that he would break his chest and die in the pulpit.

> *In Catholic countries, the sixteenth and seventeenth centuries were "Jesuit centuries". But this pervasive presence caused a reaction; by the eighteenth century the Jesuits had many enemies.*

The Downfall of the Jesuits

Great storms at sea make waves on distant shores. Junípero Serra's life was thus suddenly changed by events that had their origin in Europe. In 1767 the Jesuits were expelled from the Spanish empire, and the Franciscans were designated to take over many of their missions. Junípero, who was on a two-year tour of the home missions in the northeastern mountains, was hurriedly summoned to the college of San Fernando and told that he was to become president of the former Jesuit missions of Lower California. What had happened?

After the Reformation, the Jesuits influenced profoundly the educational and missionary work of the Catholic Church. They ran schools, colleges and universities in Catholic countries. Their missionaries took the gospel to the farthest parts of the earth. Their spirituality, their practice of obedience, their way of celebrating the liturgy and the architecture of their churches set the tone of the Counter-Reformation Church. In Catholic countries, the sixteenth and seventeenth centuries were "Jesuit centuries". But this pervasive presence caused a reaction; by the eighteenth century the Jesuits had many enemies. There were those within the Church who were jealous of their success or who wanted greater variety in the style of Church life. Outside, some were the enemies of all revealed religion and are described loosely as belonging to the Enlightenment. They thought of the Society of Jesus as the strongest element in the system of superstition and priestcraft they were determined to destroy.

Unfortunately, the Jesuits gave a handle to their enemies by their refusal to change the syllabus of their educational establishments. The syllabus, the *ratio studiorum*, as it was called, had been drawn up in 1586 while Europe was in the flush of the Renaissance and when there was great enthusiasm for classical studies. To teach boys the Greek and Latin authors seemed then the highest achievement of modernity. Two hundred years later, boys were still learning mostly Greek and Latin, but their parents wanted them to study literature and science; they wanted history taught and modern languages. The Jesuit fathers refused to change anything; in fact, their *ratio studiorum* was not revised until 1832, over a hundred and fifty years too late. One can understand that this inflexible attitude on the part of the most influential teachers of the age caused frustration. There was also a fear, real or imagined, of the political power that could be exercised behind the scenes by an international organisation like the Society of Jesus. The enemies of the Jesuits leagued together. In the absolute monarchies of southern Europe, politicians aligned their policies into a common plot against the fathers and put pressure on the popes themselves to dissolve the Society of Jesus. In 1759 the king of Portugal decreed the expulsion of all Jesuits from his dominions. In 1764 France proclaimed the dissolution of the Jesuits as a religious corporation, although they were not expelled. In 1767, as already mentioned, the Jesuits were suddenly expelled from all parts of the Spanish empire. Other Catholic states—the Kingdom of Naples and the Grand Duchy of Parma—followed suit. The same Catholic monarchs then united to put pressure on the weak Franciscan pope, Clement XIV, who decreed the complete dissolution of the Society throughout the world in 1773.

> *Priests and brothers who had spent their austere lives in the service of the young and of Christian education were often treated like criminals. Altogether it was one of the most disgraceful episodes in the long history of the Church.*

The wholesale removal of teachers is an unusual way of trying to improve education. Without warning, in obedience to a royal command from which there was no appeal, hundreds and thousands of Jesuits were abruptly removed from their houses. They were often made to walk to the nearest port; aged men were not spared. Some were taken by ship to the coast of the Papal States and unceremoniously dumped upon the shore. Many died because of the harsh treatment they received. Priests and brothers who had spent their austere lives in the service of the young and of Christian education were often treated like criminals. Altogether it was one of the most disgraceful episodes in the long history of the Church. The permanent damage done to the educational system of the Catholic Church and to her foreign missions through this institutional violence is difficult to overestimate. Soon its effects were to be seen in the world Junípero sought to influence, a world freed indeed from the presence of the Jesuits but noticeably less responsive to Christianity.

CALIFORNIA

CALIFORNIA

Lower California

Lower California is a long and narrow peninsula that runs for 675 miles parallel to the western coast of Mexico, from which it is separated by the Gulf of California. The first Spanish explorers thought that it was an island, and they had heard that it was rich in silver and pearls. But when they reached it, they were disappointed; they found an arid and rocky land with little in the way of natural wealth. Sarcastically, Cortés on his journey there in 1535 called that inhospitable place *California*, a name taken from a novel of knightly exploits that was popular at the time. Earlier still the name had appeared in the eleventh-century *Chanson de Roland*, attached to a distant land associated with Africa.[1]

The Jesuits had been in California since the end of the seventeenth century, but the missions that the Franciscans took over in 1767 were not flourishing. Ever since the beginning of the colonial period, the dire effect of diseases brought to America by Europeans had been felt by native populations that were without biological immunities,[2] although the native population had not been free of disease before Christopher Columbus arrived in 1492.[3] The coming of Europeans was an ecological disaster. The spread of venereal syphilis across Europe after 1492 was probably due to contact with the New World; the native populations of Central and South America were decimated by European diseases: smallpox, typhus, malaria, cholera, measles, whooping cough and influenza. In Mexico, sporadic

localised epidemics persisted throughout the sixteenth and seventeenth centuries and ultimately produced tremendous mortality
and decrease in population. Only in the eighteenth and nineteenth
centuries were there signs of the native population rallying in numbers in some parts of Mexico. This was not the case in Lower California, however, where the population was going down to such an
extent that the agricultural production on which the missions depended was becoming impossible. Junípero Serra was not, however,
destined to stay long in that harsh land because of another political
development that had its effect on the distant colonies of European
nations.

Russia was expanding steadily eastwards during the seventeenth
and eighteenth centuries. By 1741 Russian ships had explored the
Bering Straits, and trappers had begun a lucrative trade in furs from
the northwest coast of America. Although the first Russian settlement in Alaska was not made until 1784, Russian ships were explor-
ing farther and farther down the west coast. English ships were also
busy in the area, and the Spaniards were alarmed at the prospect of
other nations settling on the west coast of America. They decided to
anticipate this by extending California northwards.

The King of Spain at this time was the vigorous Bourbon mon-
arch Charles III, who had instigated reforms in all departments of
the state. These reforms extended to the vast Spanish dominions in
America, which, in spite of the distance, had always been controlled
by Madrid. Ever since the early sixteenth century, Central and
South America had been divided into vice-kingdoms, each under a
viceroy appointed by the king. The constant concern of Spain was
that senior administrators should come from the mother country
and return to it at the end of their term of office, to prevent the
creation of local oligarchies, with their tendency to corruption. A
striking example of this was the *residencia*, "a mandatory investiga-
tion of an official's conduct during his time of office which was held
after he had left his position. He was compelled to deposit the

equivalent of one year's salary to be used to meet possible claims against his administration."[4]

In 1765 Charles III despatched Count de Gálvez to Mexico as Inspector General with wide powers. Joseph de Gálvez was a man of humble origins who had studied law at the University of Salamanca. He had come to the notice of the king, who appointed him to the Council of Indies at Madrid, the department that controlled all the Spanish colonies in the New World. Gálvez had the mandate of overhauling the entire administration, removing unsatisfactory officials and paying special attention to increasing the revenues of the Crown. During the six years of his visitation, the energetic Gálvez achieved a great deal. Under him corrupt practices were curtailed and faulty officials brought to justice. Crown monopolies were strengthened and new ones introduced, including the profitable monopoly on tobacco. The royal revenues in New Spain began to increase steadily.

> *What Gálvez and Serra envisaged was a chain of missions running all the way up to Monterey, supported by the labour of those natives who were willing to accept baptism and guarded by a garrison of four or five soldiers at each mission.*

It was Gálvez who set his mind to solving the problem of securing for Spain the west coast of America. Because of the small number of immigrants from Spain, effective colonisation of new territories was difficult, but Gálvez found the answer in the Franciscan missions of the Sierra Gorda type, combined with a minimal number of Spanish soldiers. He picked the right man to direct the operation, Junípero Serra, and he summoned the *padre presidente* of Lower California to a conference with him. They met from October 1768 to January 1769 and planned the operation down to the last detail. During the sixteenth century, European navigators had charted the coast of present-day California. They had discovered and named San Diego and Monterey. However, the stupendous natural harbour of San Francisco had not been located because its narrow entrance, spanned today by the Golden Gate Bridge, is often covered by fog and invisible from the sea. What Gálvez and Serra envisaged was a chain of missions running all the way up to Monterey, supported by the labour of those natives who were willing to accept baptism and guarded by a garrison of four or five soldiers at each mission. A handful of priests and soldiers could thus extend Spain's colonial empire for more than six hundred miles and block Russian expansion southwards. It was a daring undertaking, but it worked; thus was modern California created.

The 1769 Expedition

The little port of San Blas on the Mexican mainland was to be the base for supplying the new colony. Count de Gálvez supervised the departure with his usual energy; he ordered the flagship *San Carlos* to be unloaded so that he could examine its keel, as a result of which he decided to have it repaired and caulked. As there was no tar for this, with this own hand he extracted gum from the *pitayos*, the tree cactus, so as to caulk the ship. He also helped Fr. Junípero pack everything the missionaries would need, including articles for saying Mass, vestments, sacred vessels and thuribles; unfortunately, he forgot the incense. Junípero had to write later to Fr. Palóu, "Please send us a little packet of incense."[5]

The expedition was led by the *San Carlos*, which set sail in January 1769, followed by the *San Antonio* in February. The land forces were in two columns, the second of which was led by the commander general of the expedition, Don Gaspar de Portolá. In June the supply ship *San José* set sail from San Blas with the stores and equipment that were going to be necessary for the combined Spanish force, once it had assembled at San Diego.

Fr. Serra was with the second land expedition, which had set out in March; unfortunately, his left leg was so swollen and painful that he had to stay behind and catch up later. The trouble with his leg, first noticed when he walked to Mexico City in 1749, had become permanent. It is probable that he suffered from varicose veins before he came to America, since this is a common complaint among monks and nuns who stand or kneel in prayer for long periods and whose sleep is interrupted by the night office, thus preventing sufficient rest. Varicose veins and swelling of the ankles were aggravated in Junípero's case by an ulcer that could have been caused initially by an insect bite, as recounted above. The infection would have become chronic in a hot climate, without proper disinfection, and it would have formed a varicose ulcer, which is extremely painful. Even in May, when Junípero caught up with the expedition, he was not well and had to be lifted onto a mule and also helped to dismount. The commander suggested that they make a stretcher so that Junípero Serra could be carried, but this made him feel annoyed at being such a nuisance to everybody. Earnestly he asked God to improve his leg, and then, typically, he called one of the muleteers and asked him to prepare a remedy. The muleteer said, "I am a muleteer, not a surgeon, I have only healed the sores of animals." Junípero Serra said to him, "Son, think of me as an animal and make the same remedy you would apply to one of your mules." So the muleteer crushed tallow between two stones and mixed it with herbs from the surrounding countryside. Then he fried the mixture and applied it to the foot and leg as a poultice, binding it up with a bandage. Junípero Serra slept well, and next morning he said Mass and was able to go on the expedition.

After the column had left the last of the missions in Lower California, it advanced into the unknown. Junípero was excited. He was fifty-six years old; at last he was experiencing what he had always wanted; he was coming with his friars to a pagan people, bringing the message of salvation, the Christian gospel, to which he had devoted his life completely since he became a Franciscan, thirty-eight years previously. Junípero kept a journal of the column's progress from 28 March to 1 July 1769. The group moved slowly because it was accompanied by a herd of two hundred cattle for stocking the missions. Junípero was filled with admiration at this new and unexplored country. He wrote: "[T]here are flowers in abundance and beautiful ones. . . . [W]hen we came to our stopping place, we met the queen of flowers—the Rose of Castile. While I write this, I have in front of me a cutting from a rose-tree with three roses in full bloom, others opening out and more than six unpetaled: blessed be He who created them!"[6]

Junípero was looking forward eagerly to seeing his first pagan natives, but when he did he commented: "I saw something I could not believe when I had read of it, or had been told about it. . . . They were entirely naked, as Adam in the [G]arden [of Eden], before [the Fall]. . . . We spoke a long time with them, and not for one moment, while they saw us clothed, could you notice the least sign of shame in them for their own lack of dress."[7] He wondered, with some apprehension, what the women would be like, but the first encounter brought reassurance because they were decently clothed.

However, he discovered that some natives did take more getting used to:

> We found an old Indian man, just as naked as all the rest. We treated him kindly and gave him to eat. . . . It was evident that he cared not a whit about anybody or anything. In fact while he was in conversation with us, right in the middle of the crowd he squatted down and, not having any clothes to bother about, right then and there attended to nature while still continuing to speak with us; and he remained just as calm as he was so relieved.[8]

Perhaps the other natives found the old man odd, too!

At one point, the Spaniards tried to establish contact with some natives, "But they disappeared, leaving a bow and a good handful of arrows. . . . I admired the beauty and clever workmanship of their flints, and the variety and the vividness of the colors along the painted shafts."[9] Fr. Serra was soon to discover the lethal accuracy with which the natives used these Stone Age weapons.

At last, on 1 July, Junípero's column arrived at the fine harbour of San Diego, today one of the bases of the United States Pacific Fleet. The two ships, *San Carlos* and *San Antonio*, were riding at anchor, and the first land column had been there since early June. From Loreto, Junípero had covered a distance of 650 miles, much of it over unknown territory. No wonder he was pleased to see the four other Franciscans and the soldiers and sailors of the expedition. "It was a day of much rejoicing and merriment for all, because even the labors themselves which each one had suffered in their respective journeys gave occasion for this through the relief of mutually relating them to one another."[10] There had been troubles enough, especially for the sailors, many of whom had died from scurvy and more of whom were continuing to die every day.

The hold of the Spaniards on this new territory was minimal. Commander de Portolá decided to leave forty members of the expedition at San Diego with Fr. Junípero and two friars to await the arrival of the *San José*, which was due any day. The *San Antonio* would sail back to San Blas for more supplies. Meanwhile, Portolá and seventy of his men with two other friars would begin the long trek north to locate the port of Monterey, 350 miles from San Diego. They left on 14 July 1769 and advanced into a vast and beautiful land. Along the sea is a coastal range of steep hills, rising to five thousand feet in places; these hills are largely composed of earth, as Junípero had noted with surprise in his journal,[11] and they are covered with a thick scrub, known as *chaparral*. In the southern part of the coast the common cactus flourishes, with its spines finer than needles. Tiny hummingbirds, the size of a butterfly, sip nectar from flowers; and the scrub jay, with plumage of bright metallic blue, utters its mocking cry. Overhead, riding effortlessly on the air currents, turkey vultures wheel and turn. Most of the missions created by the Spaniards were in this coastal area of California, which has one of the most agreeable climates of the world, with long summers and mild winters. During the day fresh breezes blow inland from the ocean; at night the air from the hills brings the scent of aromatic plants, the creosote bush, the bur sage and the desert lavender.

The San Diego Novena

Meanwhile, Junípero and the others stayed at San Diego in makeshift huts and attempted to establish friendly contacts with the local population. The first results were not encouraging. The natives stole everything they could lay their hands on and even climbed onto the ship to cut strips off its sails. When the Spaniards resisted, the natives discharged a hail of arrows that demonstrated their effectiveness; the Spaniards then showed the power of their muskets so that several people on both sides were killed or wounded. Fr. Juan Vizcáino had taken refuge in a hut with Fr. Serra; unwisely, he drew back the rug over the entrance to see how the fight was going, and immediately his hand was transfixed by an arrow. Then a Spanish lad from Mexico, who had come as a personal attendant to the friars, rushed in, his throat pierced by an arrow, fell at Junípero's feet, crying, "Father, absolve me, for the Indians have killed me", and shortly he expired. The friars' robes were covered with blood; it was their baptism of fire. No wonder Fr. Vizcáino did not take to California; the following year he returned to Mexico City and eventually went back to Spain.

Portolá's expedition was back by 24 January 1770, having covered six hundred miles. It had missed the port of Monterey but had found instead the natural harbour where San Francisco now stands, a much greater asset to California's future. One of the friars on this expedition was Fr. Juan Crespí, a native of Palma in Majorca. He was the diarist, and the meticulous account of what he saw, measured and counted on this journey is precious today as the first detailed description of California and its native peoples. The Spaniards had prospected a goodly land and had seen what could be made of it, but they found in San Diego a situation that was beginning to deteriorate. Fr. Junípero had not made a single convert, and the *San José* had not appeared. It was never heard of again and was presumed lost at sea with all its crew. The expedition was therefore entirely without news and was running short of food.

> *Portolá pointed out that if they ran out of stores they would end up with seventy Spanish corpses on the seashore, and where would hope get them then?*

February passed without any change. Portolá decided that they would all have to return to Mexico. Junípero was appalled. This meant abandoning what he knew in his heart to be his life's work. He pleaded with the governor to have hope in God. Portolá pointed out that if they ran out of stores they would end up with seventy Spanish corpses on the seashore, and where would hope get them then? Junípero begged the governor to turn to St. Joseph, patron of the expedition, and so it was decided that there should be nine consecutive days of special prayers to God, through the intercession of St. Joseph, preceding his feast day. Such "novenas" were popular with the Spaniards, and Junípero prayed as he had never done before and made sure that the whole expedition joined in.

Each day he went up the hill that dominates the San Diego harbour to look for a sail at sea, but each day he was disappointed. Finally March 19 came, and it looked as if it would be just like the days before. In fact, there was nothing at all to be seen, because of fog over the ocean. Then in the afternoon the mists parted, and there was a ship in full sail. It was the *San Antonio* on its way back from Mexico. It took four more days before it came into the San Diego harbour, but the very fact that it had been seen made Portolá stay his hand. The ship brought supplies, reinforcements and skilled workmen. There was a letter, too, from Gálvez, encouraging Portolá to go on with the settlement as planned. The Californian expedition had been saved.

The First Missions

By June 1770, Fr. Junípero Serra had moved up to Monterey, which later became the capital of Spanish California. He became *padre presidente*, the superior of the friars and of the Californian missions. At Pentecost he and Commander de Portolá formally took possession of the land and established the mission. Bells had been hung from an oak tree and were rung as the soldiers fired their rifles; from the sea, came the roar of the ship's cannon. A gigantic cross was set up and the standard of the king of Spain unfurled. Fr. Serra celebrated a High Mass and then intoned the *Te Deum*, after which there was a banquet on the beach for everyone. The mission at Monterey was dedicated to San Carlos (St. Charles Borromeo). A *presidio* was built, that is, the barracks for the small garrison that was established in each of the missions. The military commander of the expedition, Don Gaspar de Portolá, then relinquished command to Governor Pedro Fages and sailed back to Mexico City, where the church bells rang out at the command of the viceroy to celebrate the foundation of a new Spanish colony, an outpost of Christendom.

The next three years were spent in establishing a framework for the mission settlement in California. Five missions were established in this first stage. In addition to San Diego and San Carlos, there were San Antonio and San Gabriel, both founded in 1771, and San Luis Obispo, founded in 1772. Sometimes the friars changed the original location of a mission. Thus, after a year Fr. Serra decided to move

Flowerbeds decorate the yard of Mission San Diego de Alcala, in San Diego, California. This mission, established by Franciscans led by Fr. Junípero Serra in 1769, is the oldest of the California missions.

Mission San Carlos away from the *presidio* of Monterey, which was on sandy soil, sometimes flooded by sea water and distant from native settlements. He established it on good land six miles away, near the Carmel River, the other side of the promontory that juts out into Monterey Bay. Probably Fr. Serra was also relieved to move the friars and the natives away from the immediate proximity of the soldiers at the *presidio*.

In each place, two friars were stationed; they started to convert and baptise the natives and then to establish them in community. The beginnings were slow. A year after his coming to Monterey, Junípero had registered only twenty baptisms. From the beginning he emphasised the importance of communication. He writes, "[T]here are four big boys who are not only able to say their prayers well, but are making much progress in the Castilian tongue; and I, as best I can, am learning from them, as my teachers, the language of this country." [12] Language was a problem because of the large number of native languages; each of the first five missions was in an area that spoke a different language. It has been estimated that there were more than fifty different languages spoken by the natives in the area covered by present-day California. Inevitably in such circumstances, Spanish became the common idiom, although Junípero always insisted that his friars should learn the language of their area, and in some missions the catechism was translated into the local language.

Two Civilisations

The natives of California, unlike those of the Sierra Gorda, had had no previous contact with Europeans. Their number has been estimated as between one hundred thousand and three hundred thousand, the recent tendency among historians being to revise the number upwards. They lived in villages and indulged in bloody

Statue of Fr. Serra in front of Mission San Gabriel

conflict with neighbouring tribes. They were hunters, foragers and scavengers, but without the advantage of metal tools, since their technology was that of the Stone Age; as hunters they ranged widely in the forests that covered the central valley of California; further east rose the glittering peaks that the Spaniards called the "Snowy Mountains", after their own *Sierra Nevada* in Andalusia.

Within the villages, there was a high degree of social organisation. The women were skilled at weaving grasses and made baskets from these so beautifully that they were as watertight as pots. These could be used for cooking by placing in them stones that had been heated in the fire and were then dipped into the porridge of ground acorns that was a staple diet. Game was plentiful and ranged from antelope to rabbits. Along the coast, the villagers had developed boat making; their canoes could carry up to twelve men, and from these canoes they fished with great skill. In colder areas, huts were made of a circle of branches set into the ground and tied together in the centre to form a conical structure. When these became infested with vermin, they would be burned and a new hut built on a neighbouring site. The men used a kind of sauna. In an airtight wooden hut called a *temescal*, they would crowd around a fire and work up a heavy sweat; then they would rush out into the sea or a nearby lake or river.

The Spaniards brought with them a different civilisation based on agriculture and stock-rearing. They had an Iron Age technology as it was before the discovery of steam power. Their greatest single advantage was the firearm, which ensured that a handful of soldiers could control a large native population; but the natives were surprised to see how clumsy the Spaniards were in a natural setting, how they frightened wildlife by making a lot of noise, how they

The Mission San Carlos Borromeo del Rio Carmelo was built in Carmel in 1770, the second of nine missions to be founded by Father Junípero Serra along the California coast. The mission architecture has a mix of Mexican and Spanish influences.

regularly got lost and did not recognise signs that indicated paths and directions. Junípero for his part rated the land and its people much higher than Lower California. He wrote: "[T]he missions to be founded in these parts will enjoy many advantages over the old ones, as the land is much better and the water supply is more plentiful. The Indians especially of the west coast seem to me much more gifted; they are well set up, and the Governor looks upon most of them as likely Grenadier Guards because they are such stoutly built and tall fellows." [13]

As in the Sierra Gorda, the programme of the Franciscan fathers aimed at setting up a Christian community of natives, as separate as possible from the surrounding villages. The Californian natives were so attached to their former life, however, that they had to be allowed five weeks each year when they could go back to their beloved forests. The rest of the time, their work was organised on a communal basis, as was their prayer time. Junípero describes the life at Mission Carmel thus: "They pray twice daily with the priest in Church. . . . They work at all kinds of mission labor, such as farm hands, herdsmen, cowboys, shepherds, milkers, diggers, gardeners, carpenters, farmers, irrigators, reapers, blacksmiths, sacristans. . . ." [14]

Junípero gave great attention to the furnishing of the mission churches because the natives were so responsive to sound and colour. At Mission San Gabriel, "when the Fathers showed [the Indian women] a beautiful painting of the Most Blessed Mary, artistically executed, which they had brought with them, and had placed in the Church, they were so taken with it that they could not tear themselves away from it. They went to their homes and came back loaded down with seeds and provisions, which they offered to the holy image, leaving their offerings in front of the altar." [15]

Junipero's missionary method was always "on the feast of any Mystery or feast of particular importance . . . to sing the Mass, and

Bell in frame at Mission San Carlos Borromeo

divine service . . . conducted with all conceivable solemnity in order to make a deep impression, even through the eyes, on our poor convert Indians." [16] Within a fortnight of the taking possession of Monterey, Junípero was very pleased to officiate at the first procession of the Blessed Sacrament. He describes how, on 14 June 1770, "[a]fter the Mass there was a procession, in which His Sacramental Majesty passed over the ground that until then had been so heathen and miserable." [17]

Isolation

Undergirding the work of the missions was the commitment of the Franciscan friars. They were prepared to live in great isolation from one another and from the civilisation they knew. Sometimes Junípero complained about the isolation. "[I]t is childish to pretend that what I have had to put up with, and what I now endure, is any mere trifle. Where distances are so great, hardships must be faced. . . . If at any time I am called upon to mention what I find hard, it is this: I find it hard—a sinner like me—to be left all alone, with the nearest priest more than eighty leagues away, and in between nothing but savages and rough roads." [18]

As well as feeling deprived by being unable to go to confession, Junípero was often prevented from saying Mass because the wine had run out. He mentions that until the next supply ship arrives, Mass will be said only on Sundays by many of the friars, and he describes it as an unbearable deprivation. [19] Because of their strict interpretation of the rubrics of the Roman Missal requiring two candles at Mass, the friars were also prevented in the early days from saying Mass when they had no candles, but this ceased once the beehives at the missions provided wax. [20]

When writing to the missionary college in Mexico City, Junípero would ask for news about a Christian world from which he felt entirely cut off. Who was the new pope? Had the beatification of Brother Joseph de Cupertino gone through? Letters from Mexico

City came only once a year with the supply ship for California, and the same ship, when it sailed back, provided the only opportunity for writing home. There were no newspapers or means of communication. It is difficult for us to imagine such conditions of life, but for Junípero this additional hardship was something to offer up to God in the great cause to which he had devoted his life. Leaving his homeland had been hard enough; he did not want anything to be a substitute. He explained this once to his Capuchin nephew, back in Majorca: "My not answering the various letters I have received from Your Reverence was not due on my part to any lack of affection for you. When I left my country which was so dear to me, I made up my mind to leave it not merely in body alone. . . . [I]f I was continually to keep before my mind what I had left behind, of what use would it be to leave it at all?" [21] From Junípero's point of view, this sacrifice did not mean a lack of affection; on the contrary, it created a greater spiritual unity in spite of the distance. He wrote in the same letter: "[E]very day, during the holy Sacrifice of the Mass most especially, do I commend to God my one and only, and dearest sister Juana, your mother, and her children, and in particular my Capuchin." [22]

The first buildings of the missions were primitive, made of wood and earth with dried grass for the roof; of course, they leaked when it rained. Then the friars taught the natives how to make *adobe* bricks, that is, bricks made from clay and straw. They were large and heavy, shaped in wooden moulds that produced a brick about twenty-three inches long, eleven inches wide and two to five inches thick. These were baked in the sun and used to build walls and arches, which had to be low and thick to support their own weight.

These early buildings had thatched roofs, which were prone to catch fire, either by accident or through attacks from the natives. San Luis Obispo was burned down three times in the ten years that followed its foundation by Fr. Junípero; not surprisingly, the fathers at San Luis decided to manufacture the semicircular clay tiles,

An old psalter, or hymnal, printed and illuminated by hand
on sheepskin vellum, at Mission San Antonio de Padua

characteristic of Mediterranean architecture, to give a safer covering to their buildings. The clay was applied to a smooth cylindrical shape, like a tree trunk, and sun-baked; then it was fired in a wood-burning kiln. This method was so successful that by the time of Junipero's death in 1784 all the missions had tiled roofs.

We need to remember that almost all the buildings of the Californian missions we see today are later than Fr. Serra's time; most of them were built under Fr. Francisco de Lasuén, his successor as *padre presidente*. The only exception is the old chapel at San Juan Capistrano, which, by its small size, gives us an idea of the poverty of the first missions. It is called "Fr. Serra's church" and is the only building still standing where we can be sure that Blessed Junípero once said Mass.

Agricultural production was necessary to the success of the missions. It supported the life of the community, because all the natives who lived at the missions came together three times a day for their meals. After morning Mass, they sat down at long wooden tables and ate the hot corn mush that was ladled into wooden bowls. At noon, there was hot *pozole*, a stew made from corn and other vegetables, to which meat was added on special days. In the evening there was corn mush again, eaten with bread. Mission San Antonio was especially rich in wheat production and benefited from irrigation; clay pipes brought water from the San Antonio River three miles away. The water-powered mill at San Antonio was the first one in California, and it produced flour for the mission. However, the production of enough food was a problem in the early days when the numbers in the mission gradually increased. Sometimes the spot chosen for a field was not suitable, as Junípero describes in the case of Monterey: "We made a little garden nearby, and enclosed it; the Indians did the digging. The whole of it became one seeding bed. . . . Everything came out fine, but nothing grew to maturity. We were all greatly puzzled. Later we found out that the ground, while showing no signs of it, at times is washed over by the salt water of the bay, and so is fit for nothing but nettles and reeds." [23] Even when the whole mission was moved to a better site, there were occasions when the harvest failed and the friars had no alternative but to ask the natives to go out and forage for food, either in the forest or on the seashore. The herds of cattle could provide dairy products, but these were indigestible to the native Californians, who were not used to them in their customary diet as hunters, foragers and gatherers.

Raising livestock became one of the main industries of the missions. Starting with eighteen head of cattle, which was the allocation made to each mission at its foundation, the herds multiplied greatly. Indian cowboys were taught to ride so that they could round up, herd and rope the cattle. By the time of Fr. Junípero's death in 1784, the nine missions in California had 5,384 head of cattle, 5,629 sheep and 4,294 goats. At its peak, long after the death of Junípero, a mission like San Gabriel had 16,500 cattle and 1,200 horses on its extensive pastures. The missions also produced thousands of bushels of wheat, as well as beans, peas, lentils, barley and corn (maize).

Poor Examples

There was one major difficulty that faced the Franciscans in their work in California: their relation to the military governor and his troops. The presence of the soldiers was necessary because of the danger that missionaries felt in their isolation among a large pagan population. Junípero describes how in the early days four soldiers were on sentry duty every night, one every three hours. (In later years there was a sufficient number of Christian natives to ensure the defence of the missions.) These soldiers created a problem because of their misbehaviour. They did not have their wives with them and regularly went after native women. There was a disgraceful incident once when some soldiers lassoed a native woman.

Candle Shop at Mission Santa Barbara

Junípero complained, too, of the cruelty of the soldiers towards the natives. On one occasion, the soldiers ran amok after the natives had killed and eaten horses that had strayed into their territory, many miles from the *presidio*. The soldiers wreaked vengeance indiscriminately, hanging and butchering some, disembowelling and castrating others.

It was counterproductive to the work of the friars, preaching a gospel of gentleness and love, to have the bad example of Christian Spaniards so often to hand. One time, at least, it was the natives who gave the example of which Junípero could be proud: "In San [Juan] Capistrano . . . soldiers, without any restraint or shame, have behaved like brutes towards the Indian women. It may well be brought up as a reproach to Christian men, that some of the women, both gentile and convert-Christian, would not consent to what they know to be evil, even though they were enticed to it by gifts and they are themselves subject to the same passions." [24]

Another constant cause of conflict was that the careful plans made by Gálvez and Serra for the missions had not included a clear enough distinction between the respective authority of the governor and the Franciscan fathers. The latter claimed that the natives, once baptised, were under their exclusive authority, but in fact the soldiers kept on interfering with the life of the missions. This lessened the credibility of the missionaries. Junípero complained about this to the governor time and time again, but he rarely obtained support.

Appeal to the Viceroy

By the summer of 1772, Fr. Serra had had enough, and he decided that the only thing to do was to appeal to the viceroy in Mexico, over the head of the governor in California. On 20 October of that year he set sail from San Diego, and he arrived at Mexico City early in February of 1773. He was described on arrival at San Fernando's missionary college as looking worn, haggard and very thin. He had been ill on the way, running a high temperature, and had been given the Anointing of the Sick; however, once in Mexico City he lost no time in seeking an audience with the viceroy.

Fray Don Antonio María Bucareli y Ursua, Bailiff of the Order of St. John of Jerusalem, had become viceroy in 1771, after the departure of the expedition to California. He was glad, therefore, to have the opportunity of talking to someone who had firsthand knowledge of the new colony, because its very existence was under threat from the Spanish administration. The royal government in Madrid was making regular demands for greater economy, and so far California had been a source of expense and not of income. It was proposed to close down the port of San Blas for a start and to send supplies by mule trains instead. Serra had been flabbergasted to learn this when he had passed through San Blas. He thought it utterly impractical. Now he was prepared to devote all his experience and his zeal to persuading the viceroy of the error of such a course. His presence in Mexico City at this juncture was providential; as at San Diego in 1770, his intervention changed the course of events.

It was fortunate for Junípero that Bucareli was viceroy. Not only was he one of the best examples of a Spanish administrator, incorruptible, conscientious, aware of the needs of the people and probably the most able viceroy Mexico ever had. He was also a member of a lay religious order and thus able to appreciate Serra's religious motivation. Bucareli had become a full member of the Order of St. John of Jerusalem, also known as the Knights of Malta, when he took the three vows of poverty, chastity and obedience in 1741 at the age of twenty-four. The Order had been founded at the time of the Crusades as a group of Hospitallers who nursed sick pilgrims. Later it took on a military character to defend the Holy Land against

PAGE 76   *Clay bricks dry in the sun for the building of adobe structures, as part of an outdoor exhibit at El Presidio de Santa Barbara State Historic Park in California.*

PAGE 77   *Example of tile roofing at Mission Santa Barbara*

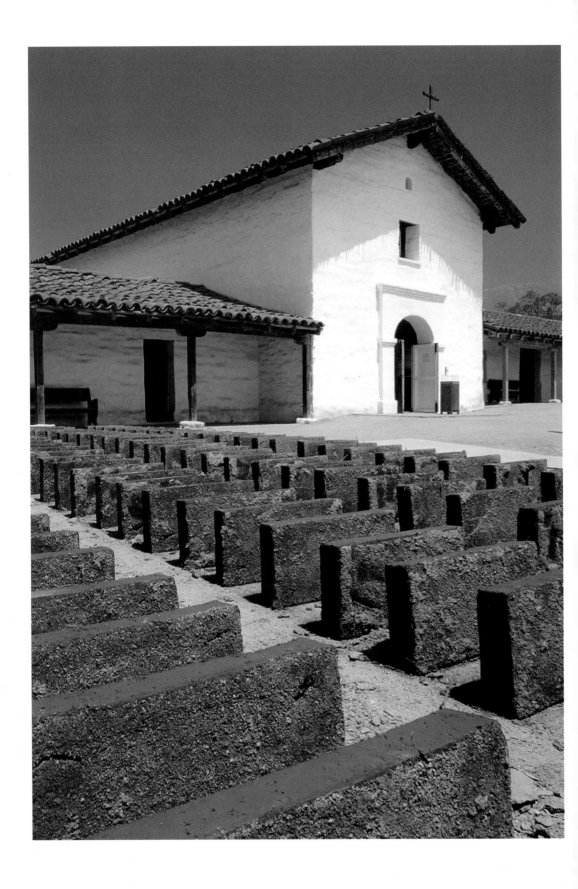

Portrait of Viceroy Antonio María Bucareli

attack. By the eighteenth century it operated a fleet from its great fortress of Valletta in Malta and tried to keep the Mediterranean clear of pirates for the shipping of Christian nations. Several of its members also entered the service of Catholic monarchs, the best known being Bailiff Pierre de Suffren, the French admiral who fought against the British in India during the War of American Independence. Bucareli had been in the army of the king of Spain before becoming governor of Cuba. He was devoid of personal ambition and had hoped to return to Spain. While in Mexico, he tried to retire, but Charles III prolonged his term of office so that he was still viceroy at the time of his death in 1779.

New Regulations

Bucareli gave Serra a positive interview and asked him to write down all his recommendations for the California missions. This Junípero did under thirty-two headings in a long memorandum dated 13 March 1773. The key issue was dealt with in number 9:

> Your Excellency should notify the said Officer and the soldiers that the training, governance, punishment and education of baptized Indians or of those who are being prepared for Baptism, belong exclusively to the Missionary Fathers, the only exception being for capital offenses. Therefore no chastisement or ill-treatment should be inflicted on any of them whether by the Officer or by any soldier, without the Missionary Father's passing upon it.[25]

Another crucial request was that any soldier who gives bad example should be removed when this is requested by a missionary father, although the reason for this cannot always be given, for instance, if it is because of sexual misconduct.

Junípero also had many recommendations for the improvement of the links between the port of San Blas and the struggling settlements in California. He suggested measures that would attract adequate labourers to the missions and also promote settlers. He went into detail about the need for a doctor, carpenters and a

blacksmith and for the provision of authenticated weights and measures so that supplies were up to their specification. He also included compassionate requests for the moving of eight soldiers who
had been away from their families for a long time. Altogether, the
long petition showed how well Junípero knew the situation and how
practical he was in assessing its needs. He ends with a comment
typical of his wry humour: "[S]o as not to stop asking for something
right to the end, I beg Your Excellency to order some small allow-
ance for the expenses of my trip." [26] During his seven months in
Mexico City, Junípero went to see the viceroy several times and had
long discussions with him.

> *Junípero was sixty-one years old by now,*
> *with ten more years to live. . . .*

The viceroy submitted the petition to his council, and Junípero
provided some elucidations at his request. Then, in August 1773, he
left Mexico City, which he was never to see again. The land journey
back to San Blas was slow because Junípero was ill; the president of
the missionary college hired a carriage to take him to the little port
that had been saved by his timely intervention. From San Blas he
sailed to San Diego and travelled overland to Carmel, which he
reached in June 1774. He was delighted to be back and noted in a
letter: "At long last, I arrived at the mission here after an absence of
one year, eight months and sixteen days, when I left it for San Diego
and Mexico." [27] He was even more pleased when the viceroy published the new *regulamento* that had been drawn up in response to

*The altar of the Serra Chapel at Mission San Juan
Capistrano is backed by an elaborate, gilded reredos
installed during the chapel's restoration.*

PAGES 82–83   *Kitchen at Mission San Carlos Borromeo*

Junípero's petition. Nearly all his requests were granted. Governor Fages was replaced, and the friars of the California mission could look forward to a new period of peaceful development for their native converts. Junípero was sixty-one years old by now, with ten more years to live; the time was marked first of all by the founding of four new missions.

Expansion

Early in 1775, the first arrangements were made for the foundation of the mission at San Juan Capistrano, and, although this was delayed by an attack on Mission San Diego, which will be mentioned shortly, the formal foundation took place on 1 November 1776; within a year the simple church of *adobe* bricks was built. It still stands today and has the honour of being California's oldest building. Capistrano soon became a flourishing mission, noted for the abundance of its fruit, pomegranates, peaches, apricots, quince, and so on. When the fathers arrived, they found the land covered with wild grapevines; they grafted vines from Lower California on this stock and soon were able to make wine for Mass and for the table.

The mission at San Francisco came next. The first Mass was said there on 29 June 1776. That was an important year for Americans, since the Declaration of Independence was proclaimed at Philadelphia five days later, on 4 July. At the time, the thirteen former English colonies on the Atlantic seaboard seemed as far from Fr. Junípero's Spanish missions as if they had been on another planet. The old Spanish church in San Francisco is called Mission Dolores, and it still stands on one of that city's busy streets.

Mission Santa Clara was founded in 1777, and the olive trees planted by the first Franciscans still grow in the cloistered gardens of the mission, now in the middle of a university campus. Harvests of grain and fruit were abundant at Santa Clara, which may explain

Dining room at Mission La Purisima

why the native population was the greatest of any of the missions; it reached 2,228 in the year 1800.

Fr. Junípero had the joy of blessing one more foundation, San Buenaventura, in 1782; its church is now a parish church of the seaside town of Ventura. In all, Fr. Serra founded nine missions in California; twelve more were added after his death, so that there were twenty-one Franciscan missions in 1823. By that time, however, the whole system was near its end, which came with secularisation ten years later.

Although there was a famine in California when Junípero returned from Mexico, this proved to be the last time there was an acute shortage of food in the colony. Not only was the arrival of stores from San Blas better regulated, but the amount produced by the missions began to increase regularly. Junípero could write to the viceroy with evident satisfaction: "[T]he fruits of our preaching are coming in, and also those from the fields." [28]

At Monterey Fr. Serra was able to spend the greater part of the day instructing catechumens. They would sit round him in a great circle, and he would explain to them, with the help of an interpreter, the truths of the Christian faith: how God had become man to save us from the miserable conditions to which sin and death had reduced the human race; how Jesus Christ had revealed by his teaching the way to God, our true happiness; how his own people had rejected him and nailed him to a cross; and how the Resurrection of Jesus had been his triumph over sin and death, manifesting our own future if we believe in Christ and enter into his community by baptism. The natives listened attentively as this new perspective was revealed to them. It made sense of all the sorrows and sufferings of life on earth. Suddenly they saw it as a preparation for true life with God, a life of bliss sharing the love of the Blessed Trinity with all the redeemed in heaven. They particularly liked the Padre's words about

Mission San Antonio de Padua

a wonderful woman called Mary, the mother of Jesus, who had taken part at the foot of cross in the suffering of her Son and now shared his risen life in heaven. They were happy to learn that she was their mother, too, that no one, however small, was beneath her consideration and that she continually prayed for them in the presence of God. Gradually, after all this had been explained and understood, the catechumens would be baptised.

> *It would be possible, travelling light, to sleep*
> *every third night in a mission along the*
> *way, strung out as they were sixty-five miles*
> *from each other. . . .*

Junípero made a habit of tracing the sign of the cross on those who came to him, and he would say to them: *Amar a Dios*, "Love God", so that these words became the usual greeting in the whole area, whenever the natives met Spaniards on the way. There was now a route running from San Diego to Monterey, which was known as *el Camino Real*, "the Royal Highway", and Junípero noted that it would be possible, travelling light, to sleep every third night in a mission along the way, strung out as they were sixty-five miles from each other. Couriers on horseback could reach a mission every night. Usually the missionaries travelled on mules. Fr. Maynard Geiger, O.F.M., the great historian of Junípero Serra, reached the conclusion, after a careful study of the evidence, that when he was in California Junípero hardly ever travelled on foot as he had done when he was in Mexico.[29] His legs were very painful at times; in a letter written in 1779 he complains that he cannot sleep because of

The courtyard at California's Mission San Juan Capistrano, "The Jewel of the Missions". Founded in 1776 by Junípero Serra, it was the seventh of twenty-one established by the Spanish Franciscans. Though in ruins, it is still famed for its lovely gardens.

the pain in his legs, and there were days when he could not say Mass. That year there was a rare occasion when he did go on foot and walked seventy miles in two days. One of the royal surgeons and some of the officers from the frigate that happened to be in Monterey harbour examined his ulcerated foot afterwards. They said that it was a miracle that he had been able to walk at all, and they proposed to start treatment, but Fr. Junípero postponed it, saying that he was too busy; later he put if off altogether, which is a pity, because when he had had his ulcer treated on the journey from Lower California it had improved dramatically.

The material progress of the missions remained subordinate to their main purpose, the conversion of the natives to Christianity and their introduction to the civilisation of the Spanish empire. The growth of the communities in the missions brought satisfaction to these dedicated Franciscans; Junípero wrote to Viceroy Bucareli: "Just to see a hundred boys and girls of about the same size, to hear them pray, and answer questions—being well versed in all the questions and answers of Christian Doctrine; to hear them sing, to see them all dressed in worsted clothes and woollens; to see how happy they are at play, and how they run up to the Father as if they had known him all their lives—all this gladdens the heart, and impels one gratefully to give praise to God." [30] It was the expansion of the Christian community that justified in the eyes of the Padre the practice, which seems heartless today, of bringing back runaways to the missions by force. It was seen as the bringing back of runaway children to boarding school. The objective reality of baptism had made them members of the Church who needed to be preserved from the occasions of grave sin, always present in the pagan way of life of the native villages. The soldiers would be required to escort one of the missionaries so as to find runaways and bring them back to the mission. Sometimes the soldiers grumbled at this, but Fray Junípero

Interior of Serra Chapel at Mission San Juan Capistrano

insisted on the serious responsibility that he carried in this regard: "[T]hese wayward sheep are my burden, and I am responsible for them not at the treasury [*tribunal de cuentas*] in Mexico but at a much higher tribunal than that."[31]

The second period of Junipero's stay in California, from 1773 to the year of his death in 1784, was not without its problems, in spite of the regularly increasing numbers and properties of the missions. In 1775 there was a sudden attack on Mission San Diego; the natives in that area had always been the most difficult of those the Spaniards had encountered in California. Because the *presidio* was short of water, the mission had been moved four miles inland during the previous year. Trouble erupted when two Christian natives were disciplined for stealing. They fled to the pagan villages, and, on the night of 4 November 1775, more than six hundred natives surrounded the mission in total silence, attacked it, burned it to the ground and killed several Spaniards, including Fray Luis Jayme. The *presidio* down by the harbour was out of earshot and unaware that anything unusual was happening. When Fr. Junípero Serra heard of the death of the thirty-five-year-old fellow Mallorquin friar, his reaction was characteristic. First of all, he gave thanks to God for the martyrdom that had occurred: "Thanks be to God, now indeed that land has been watered [with blood]; certainly now the conversion of the San Diego Indians will be achieved."[32] Second, he was concerned that the military should not mount a campaign to avenge the dead Spaniards. The new governor, Don Fernando Rivera y Moncada, was not an intelligent man, and he and Serra had been at loggerheads over practically every decision since he had arrived. Since murder was a capital offence, the decision about what should be done to the culprit who had been arrested by the Spaniards was in the hands of the governor. But in this case Junípero appealed to Bucareli: "[A]s to the murderer, let him live, in order that he should be saved—which is the very purpose of our coming here. . . . Give him to understand, after a moderate amount of punishment, that he is being pardoned in accordance with our law which commands us to forgive injuries; and let us prepare him, not for death, but for eternal life."[33] But the killings had given everyone a nasty scare and had been a reminder of how precarious the whole Californian project was.

The Back Door to California

One of the recommendations of Fr. Serra's long memorandum of 1773 had been that a line of communication should be opened up overland between California and New Mexico as a back door to California. The Spanish settlements in New Mexico went back to the sixteenth century. Although there had been several setbacks, by the end of the eighteenth century New Mexico and its capital, Santa Fe, attracted Spanish settlers to such an extent that they outnumbered the natives by four to one. The governors of New Mexico had to spend a lot of time fighting against the Apache tribes on their frontier; nevertheless, there was a richness of Spanish life about the province that would obviously greatly help California if the two could be brought into regular contact. Between New Mexico and California lies the vast mountainous desert of present-day southern Arizona and the Colorado River. West of the Colorado is a desert of sand, below sea level and intensely hot in the summer. Then comes the San Jacinto mountain range, beyond which is the coastal plain where the Franciscans had founded their missions. The Yuma people controlled the fords on the Colorado River, and it was crucial to secure their friendship if New Mexico and California were to be effectively linked.

Junípero was not the first one to suggest the creation of an overland route to California. In fact, a Franciscan called Fr. Francisco Garcés had begun the exploration of the area in 1768 and had charted part of the course of the Colorado down to the sea; it was most important, too, that he had made friends with the Yuma tribes. Encouraged by these considerations, Viceroy Bucareli

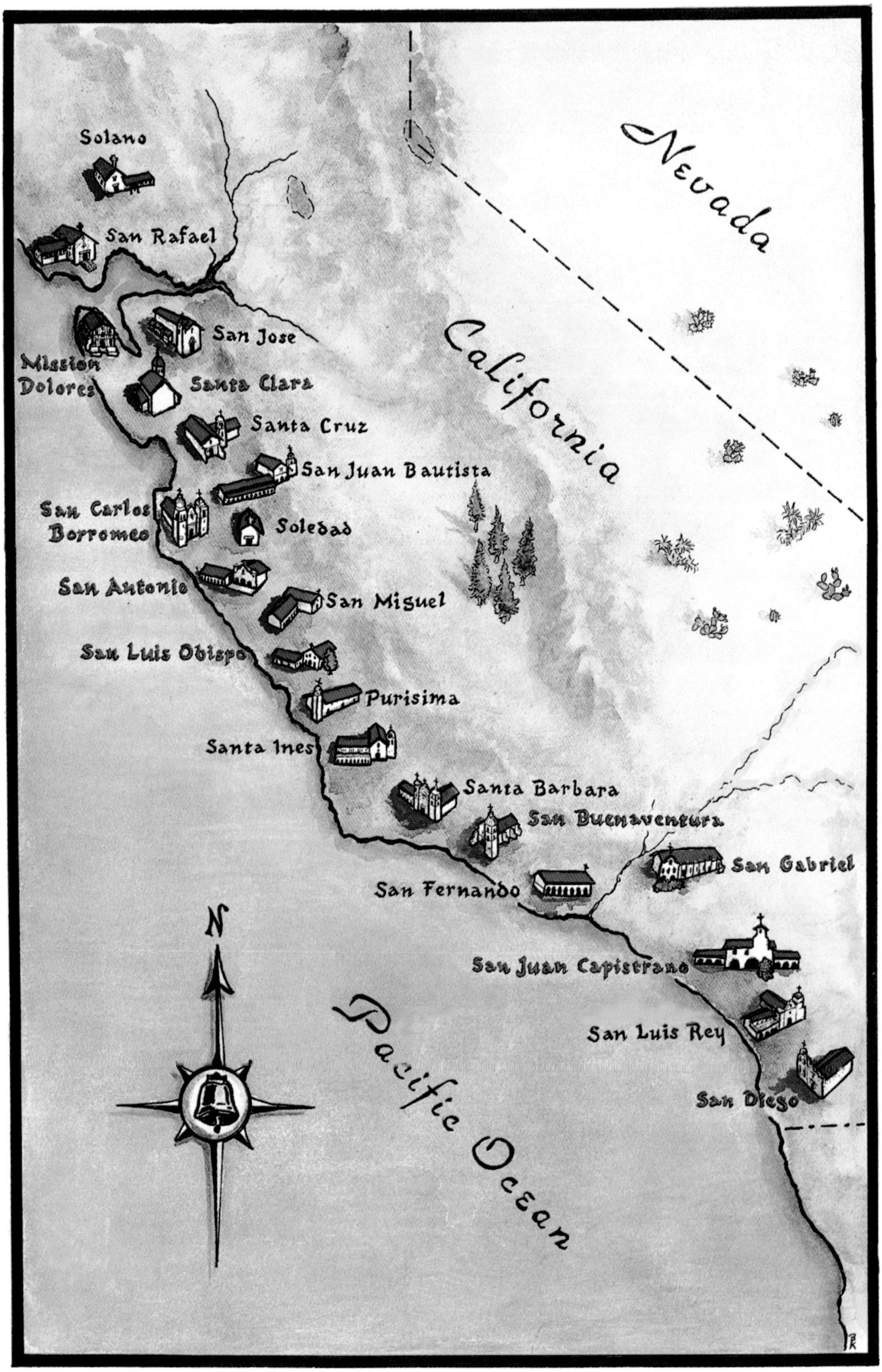

Nevada
California
Solano
San Rafael
San Jose
Mission Dolores
Santa Clara
Santa Cruz
San Juan Bautista
San Carlos Borromeo
Soledad
San Antonio
San Miguel
San Luis Obispo
Purisima
Santa Ines
Santa Barbara
San Buenaventura
San Gabriel
San Fernando
N
San Juan Capistrano
Pacific Ocean
San Luis Rey
San Diego

authorised an expedition to discover the way westwards and put in charge one of the finest of the Spanish soldiers of the time, Don Juan Bautista de Anza, an experienced frontiersman who knew the ways of the natives, since he had been born in the Sonora province of northwest Mexico. Anza had an iron will combined with practical psychology; he knew how to persuade people to his point of view. Father Garcés wrote of him: "He is extremely tolerant and patient, generous, and well-liked by the Indians. . . . I recognise in Don Juan Bautista de Anza a great fund of discretion to meet any unforeseen emergency."[34] With these qualities went the toughness of a man who could spend hours in the saddle each day and endure extreme physical conditions in the pursuit of his ideal. Anza's expedition set off in January 1774 from Tubac, Arizona, accompanied by Fr. Garcés. In the territory of the Yuma, Anza met their chief, a giant of a man called Olleyquotequiebe, whom he renamed Salvador Palma; one can see why! Anza treated Salvador with the greatest consideration and gave him a medal from the king of Spain. He knew that in Yuma society good relations depended on the giving and receiving of gifts, and he had little presents of beads and tobacco for each of the six hundred warriors who accompanied the Spaniards after they had crossed the Colorado River at the present-day town of Yuma and headed south along the river. There were many setbacks and hardships in the following weeks, when the Spaniards were on their own, turning west to cross the desert and finding their way up the steep passes of the San Jacinto mountains. Their climb brought them into an alpine climate, with forests of fir trees below snowy peaks and an abundance of springs and lakes. Eventually, on 22 March 1774, the expedition knocked on the gates of Mission San Gabriel, where the friars and soldiers gave them a big welcome.

Don Juan Bautista de Anza and Fr. Junípero Serra met that year in present-day Santa Barbara County. It was on 28 April 1774. Anza had been up to Monterey and was in a hurry to get back to Mexico to prepare his next expedition. Serra was riding north from San

Diego, after his visit to Mexico City, and asked Anza to interrupt his journey so that they could talk and share their plans. Anza, writing about the meeting, said: "I yielded"; it was not something he often did! The two parties dismounted and pitched their tents, and, after dinner, those two pioneers talked by the campfire, far into the night, about what had been achieved and what could be dreamed of for California. They were united by the same enthusiasm for the whole Spanish enterprise in North America.

Anza having demonstrated that it was possible for a party on horseback to ride from Mexico to California, the next step was to send a colonising expedition with everything necessary for a settlement on San Francisco Bay. Bucareli entrusted this second expedition to Anza too. It was a much bigger undertaking. Thirty-eight families were accompanied by ten soldiers and three Franciscans. There were muleteers and cowboys to look after 340 horses, 165 pack mules and more than 300 beef cattle, of which 100 were to be slaughtered to provide food on the way. All the gear needed for the journey and for the establishment of the new town was carried on muleback. There were 240 persons in all by the time the expedition left Tubac on 23 October 1775, and the column stretched out over a mile when it was on the move.

Those on this trek suffered from the cold, and there was a freak snowstorm in the desert, but eventually, on 4 January 1776, the expedition came down to Mission San Gabriel. Anza then led it north to prospect the site of the *presidio* on San Francisco Bay, and they gazed with wonder at the inland sea. Fr. Pedro Font, the diarist of the expedition, wrote:

> Although in my travels I saw very good sites and beautiful country, I saw none which pleased me so much as this. And I think that if it could be well settled like Europe there would not be anything more

A fountain surrounded by coloured tiles decorates the grounds at Mission San Buenaventura in Ventura, California. Only the church remains from the original mission complex.

beautiful in all the world, for it has the best advantage for founding
in it a most beautiful city, with all the conveniences desired, by land
as well as by sea, with that harbour so remarkable and so spacious in
which may be established shipyards, docks and anything that might
be wished. [35]

Thus was San Francisco founded, and Fr. Junípero had his oft-
expressed wish fulfilled that there should be Christian families in
California so "that the Indians may realize that . . . there are mar-
riages, also, among Christians." [36] He observed wittily, "[T]he
people here will now be rid of their belief that Spaniards are the
offspring of mules, a notion they previously had, seeing that mules
were the only members of the female gender they saw among us." [37]
The *pueblo* at San Francisco, the first secular town in California, was
established in June 1776.

Serra had difficult relations with all four governors of Upper California in his time, so it is a relief to know that he was not alone in
this. Anza disagreed with Governor Rivera y Moncada about practically everything, thought that he was mad and was not on speaking
terms with him when he left California to ride back over the mountains to New Mexico.

Tensions

To anyone who thinks Spanish America in the eighteenth century
was decadent and rigidly conservative, the story of California should
present a different perspective. Under the energetic Bourbon King
Charles III, changes were regularly being made in the interests of
greater economy, accountability and efficiency. One of these occurred in 1776, when California, New Mexico and the province of
Sonora were combined into a new administrative unit, known as the
Provincias Internas, under a commander general, Teodoro de Croix,
who resided at Arispe in Sonora. This change was made to provide a
unified command in view of the proposed joint development of
the area, but it had the unfortunate effect of introducing an interme-

diary between Junípero Serra and the ever-helpful viceroy in Mexico, Antonio María de Bucareli, who, as a professed member of the Order of Malta, encouraged the religious ideals of the Franciscans and their missions. Henceforth, Serra had to appeal to de Croix in his quarrels with the governor of California. Rivera had left in 1777, and the new governor, Filipe de Neve, was a quiet and efficient man; Junípero had a good impression of him to begin with, but in fact he turned out to be the most subversive of the friars' enemies. Neve had been deeply influenced by the ideas of the Enlightenment, and his view of the natives corresponded to the one popularised by the French writer and philosopher Jean-Jacques Rousseau (1712–1778). Rousseau had idealised them as "noble savages", uncontaminated by the corrupting influence of civilisation. Neve therefore did not accept the friars' view that Indians had to be treated as adult children and to be separated from the evil influences of their own native culture. Neve wanted to limit the power of the friars and to introduce a different style of Spanish settlement. He wanted a civil, as opposed to a religious, administration, and he wanted the friars to look after churches only and not to be in charge of all aspects of life, as they were in the missions of California. One friar per town would serve the church, as in any parish in Spain, and the natives would be free to run their own lives. The new system would have the advantage of not requiring two friars for each church and so would save on the expenses of the royal exchequer. In each township, the natives would elect an *alcalde* (mayor) and *regidores* (aldermen) as in Spanish municipalities, and these would administer the community.

Already in 1778 Commander General de Croix had told Fr. Junípero about the new-style settlements that were being proposed. The *padre presidente* recorded his reservations in a carefully worded letter:

> I have thought over the new plan—to set up, among these gentiles, pueblos composed of Spaniards, or of people of mixed blood, instead of increasing the number of the missions. . . . [I]t appeared to me to have many drawbacks. . . .

Missions, my Lord, missions—that is what this country needs. They will not only provide it with what is most important—the light of the Holy Gospel—but also will be the means of supplying foodstuffs for themselves and for the Royal Presidios. They will accomplish this far more efficiently than these pueblos without priests. . . .

Later on, when the gentiles that are spread throughout all these lands have become Christian, and when they are settled in their various reservations or missions . . . I assure you that then will be the proper time for introducing towns of Spaniards. Let them be of good conduct and blameless life.[38]

It is incredible that Neve drew up his far-reaching regulations without showing a draft to Fr. Serra or consulting him or other Franciscans in any way. He completed his work in 1779; by then Bucareli was dead, and there was no one to block the proposals. Croix sent them to Madrid, where they received royal assent in 1781.

When Neve notified Fr. Serra of the way in which California would be administered in the future, the *padre presidente* could not believe his ears. Here was someone, newly arrived in California and ignorant of the real situation, especially the native mentality, who was putting into position, without consulting those who had been on the spot for many years, arrangements that could spell disaster. The governor turned up at Monterey before Mass on Palm Sunday 1779 and told Fr. Serra to get on with the election of Indian *alcaldes* forthwith. Junípero lost his temper with him and was then so upset that he had to stand a long time before the altar to calm down. He could not sleep that night and cried out: " 'What is the meaning of it all, O Lord?' and a voice within me seemed to reply in very clear words: 'Be prudent as serpents and as simple as doves.' "[39]

Fr. Junípero interpreted this as meaning that he should go along with the governor's instructions and proceed with the appointment of *alcaldes*. This policy paid off, because the system soon proved unworkable. Some of the *alcaldes* were so thrilled with their elevation that they made themselves ridiculous. Another, with an eye to the main chance, started to make money by procuring women for the Spanish soldiers; another fathered a child incestuously and then fled to the mountains with a band of deserters. When the friars punished them for their misdeeds, Neve intervened, claiming that civil officers were exempt from ecclesiastical jurisdiction. Fr. Serra then quoted Bucareli's regulations of 1774 to him: all the Indians in the missions were under the authority of the fathers. Neve began to see that the application of European categories to the Californian situation had many drawbacks.

Massacre in New Mexico

The setting up of new-style *pueblos* foundered first on the opposition of the College of San Fernando in Mexico, to which all the friars ultimately owed obedience. The president of the college made it clear that if the proposed scheme were put into place in California, no further Franciscans would be available. Second, disaster in New Mexico put an end to the whole scheme. Governor General de Croix decided to start settlements on the new model in Yuma country on the Colorado. The Yuma chieftain, Salvador Palma, had already been brought to Mexico City by Anza, who stood godfather at his baptism. Palma had been presented to Viceroy Bucareli, and everything was done to encourage his friendship with Spain, since upon it depended the continuation of the trail that led westwards, the "back door to California". Palma asked for a mission to be established in his territory. Unfortunately, when the time came to put this into operation, Bucareli was dead, and Commander General de Croix was in charge; nor was Anza involved, probably because of jealousy. A column of settlers came up from Mexico without any presents for the Indians; without presents, no treaty could be concluded. The settlers drove the Yuma off their land without paying for it. Then the boneheaded Rivera arrived with another group of land-hungry settlers. Rivera did not maintain proper discipline over his soldiers, whose misbehaviour infuriated the Yumas. In July 1781 they gathered their braves stealthily without alerting the Spaniards, and, when their army was at full force, they fell upon the settlers with blood-curdling cries. Every single man was slaughtered, including Rivera and Fr. Garcés, who had first explored the region. The women and children were taken off into slavery. Junípero heard about the disaster by December of that year. Although a Spanish punitive expedition later secured the release of the captives, the "back door to California" remained permanently closed. From then on, all communications between California and Mexico had to be by sea.

". . . when we came here, we did not find even a single Christian . . ."

This disaster did, however, have one advantage. It seems to have made Neve and Croix rethink their policy about new-style *pueblos*. It also underlined the success of the Franciscans in California, even in areas such as San Diego and the Santa Barbara Channel, where the natives had a warlike character. It was not the existence of a few miserable *presidios* that could explain the relative security of those missions and their flourishing condition; it was the spiritual quality of the Franciscans, the esteem in which the padres were held and the love they had for the natives and the natives for them. Whatever Enlightenment ideas might be about the place of religion in society, it became clearer to Spanish administrators that the views of the padres about the rate of development in California should be taken into consideration. Anyone trying to understand the situation had to advert to something that soldiers and politicians did not usually take into account but which Junípero Serra spelled out in a letter to Neve: "[T]he good standing in which we [the padres] are universally regarded may be gathered from the consideration that when we

A worn wooden crucifix hangs in the rafters of San Antonio de Padua, the asistencia, *or sub-mission, to Mission San Luis Rey. It may date to the early years of the building.*

came here, we did not find even a single Christian, that we have engendered them all in Christ, that we, everyone of us, came here for the single purpose of doing them good and for their eternal salvation; and I feel sure that everyone knows that we love them." [40]

Spiritual Strength

Junípero Serra's qualities of leadership did not show themselves only in the endless sparring with the governors of California. Something far more important to the welfare of the missions was the quality of the Franciscans who worked there. The *padre presidente* often had occasion to recall the spiritual strength that was required. He never hid the hardness of the life to which the missionaries were called. Writing to Fr. Palóu, asking him to bring two friars, he said: "Those who come should be provided with a good stock of patience and charity, and their stay will be one of delight to them. It will enable them to amass riches—a wealth of sufferings." [41]

Junípero would describe the kind of recruits he expected from San Fernando College as "friends of Matins", [42] that is, friars who were not afraid of getting up at midnight to recite Matins in the college chapel. Those who were regular in attending were giving proof that they possessed the zeal and self-sacrifice needed for the missions.

When he was less than a year away from death, he wrote to the president of the college: "We need saints, saints, even though they be no more than Confessors." [43] This was a typically Serra joke; that is, slightly laboured. In the Roman Missal as used in the eighteenth century, "Confessors" was the lowest category of men saints (after Apostles, Martyrs and Doctors). But the cry for help was serious; only sanctity could avail in the work of the missions. Junípero Serra was utterly convinced of that. His personal efforts were directed towards achieving holiness because it would make him responsive to God's will and thus an effective instrument of God's saving work.

Like a good religious superior, Fr. Serra had to be attentive to the personal needs of the friars who were under his direction. They were not supermen; they needed support and encouragement in their difficult and lonely task. Junípero's skill in providing this is illustrated in a long letter he wrote to Fr. Juan Figuer in 1779. Fr. Figuer was a young friar in his thirties, originally from Aragon in Spain, who had been on the missions for eight years. In 1777 he had been sent by Fr. Junípero Serra to San Diego, which he did not like at all. There was not enough to eat, there were difficulties with the garrison and there was constant fear of an uprising among the natives, similar to the one that had occurred four years previously. Figuer did not welcome the prospect of being stuck full of stone-tipped arrows. He wrote to the *padre presidente*, saying that he wanted to resign and to go back to his cell in San Fernando.

Junípero starts his reply by telling a story he had read in a Spanish collection of anecdotes:

> One of our communities of religious had just started Matins, and before long, a friar went up to the Guardian and whispered: "Father, may I retire to my cell? I am not feeling well."
> The Superior's answer was: "Brother, for the love of God, stay in your place. I can assure you that if all in choir who are not feeling well were to leave, there would be no Matins. All of us, and I first of all, would leave." [44]

He points out, therefore, that "troubles abound everywhere—a little more here, a little less there." [45] Of course, Serra writes that he will not speak of the moral value of bearing opposition because "you should not preach to preachers" (which is precisely what he does!), but he stresses the wonderful work that Fr. Figuer is doing; surely he can hardly give it up without wondering who is going to carry it on if he leaves. But, writes Junípero, if what he says is not convincing, Figuer is entirely free to make up his own mind. Before he decides, let him remember the words of St. Paul: *Charitas Dei urget nos* (2 Cor 5:14: "the love of Christ impels us"; Serra writes *Charitas Dei* for *Charitas Christi*). Serra asks Figuer to think things over and then

let his superior know what he wants to do, and he ends: "[Y]ou are speaking to one who appreciates your difficult position, and is most eager to do all he can for your welfare and happiness." [46] This understanding approach was successful; Figuer decided to stay on at San Diego, where he remained until his peaceful demise in bed five years later.

Mutual Affection

It is more difficult to find direct evidence of the interaction of Blessed Junípero Serra and the native population. As he often stated, his attitude sprang from the love he had for them and for his concern for their eternal salvation. What was the attitude of the natives to him? On one occasion he was deeply moved by their spontaneous expression of affection. He was travelling along the coast of the Santa Barbara Channel; the track led along the beach, but the waves were so big that it was impossible to follow it. Junípero had to follow steep and muddy paths up the hills. He described how

> tears welled up into my eyes when I saw with what good will [these poor gentiles] came to my assistance, linking me on both sides by the arm to get me over the muddy steep hills, which I could not negotiate either on foot or on horseback. . . . What a pleasure it was for me to see them, in great numbers, walking along the road with me, and breaking out into song each time I started a tune for them to take up. When the first batch took its leave, a second group, watching out for the opportunity, would come up for me to make the sign of the Cross upon their foreheads. Some followed me many days. [47]

The grieving of the natives after Junípero's death was another indication of the high regard in which they held him. They could not mistake his unconditional love for them, which is illustrated by the following episode recorded by Palóu:

> Four days before his death . . . an old Indian woman of over eighty years of age, a neophyte, came in. . . . [Junípero Serra] rose and,

Gardens of Mission San Diego

going into the little room where he slept, brought out a bed-blanket and gave it to the old woman. Smilingly I said to him: "Is she going to pay you for the chickens?" He joined me in the merriment and answered "Yes" . . . [W]hen this Indian woman was still a pagan, shortly after the foundation of Mission San Carlos, and the mission had only one hen with its chicks (which were intended for propagating the brood) she instructed her little grandson to kill the chicks with his bow, as he did. They both shared in the meal of young chickens. Since she had been found out in the theft, she received the nickname "the old chicken woman". This was the reason for our laughter. Nevertheless he practiced the act of charity above described; and that action, so replete with charity, was the reason why at his death there was found nothing more over his bed of bare boards than a half blanket.[48]

It is very significant that, towards the end of his life, Junípero criticised the phrase *gentes de razón*, "the reasonable people", which was commonly used of the Spaniards, "as if the Indians did not have the use of reason too".[49] This was a far cry from the attitude of most Spanish settlers.

Administering Confirmation

Although Fr. Junipero's normal place of residence was Mission San Carlos Borromeo at Carmel, he had visited all the Californian missions as *padre presidente*, and more especially from 1778 onwards, when he had been given the faculty of administering confirmation, the sacrament of anointing with chrism that completes the effect of baptism and gives to a Christian the gifts of the Spirit that are needed by an active witness to Christ. In the Eastern Churches, this anointing is given by a priest immediately after baptism; in the Western Church, the bishop is the normal minister of confirmation, which is administered once a child has reached a certain sense of responsibility. When Junípero was in Lower California, he learned that the faculty of giving confirmation had been given to the Jesuit

Covered walkway at Mission San Carlos Borromeo

fathers by the pope because no bishop was able to visit these distant missions. Junípero therefore applied to Rome for such a faculty in 1768, while he was still in Lower California. The request was processed with agonising slowness. The permission was granted by the Roman authorities in 1776, but, because of the *patronato real*, it had to be authorised by the king of Spain and the Royal Council of the Indies at Madrid and then forwarded to America. It did not reach Fr. Serra until 1778. He was delighted to receive this faculty at last, and he tells us that he started by confirming ninety children on the feast of SS. Peter and Paul "and in a very solemn manner".[50] A careful record was kept in the missions of the names of those confirmed, as of every baptism, marriage and burial. By 1784 Junípero notes proudly that he had confirmed 5,275 persons.

His last tour of the missions took place in the first half of 1784. He administered confirmation and checked on the spiritual and material welfare of his nine foundations. Their condition gave him a great deal of satisfaction; he wrote to the president of the College of San Fernando: "I have just finished my round of visitations from San Diego to San Francisco. Nowhere at all—and I speak in all sincerity—have I found anything to criticize. All the ministers are busily engaged in their work both spiritual and temporal. And San Fernando may well be very proud of them."[51]

However, the special permission given by Rome for a priest to give confirmation expired in July 1784. An application had been made for its renewal, but this did not receive a reply until after Junípero's death. He was conscious that his time on earth was drawing to a close and had written in 1783: "[T]he nearness of my own death is constantly before me; more especially as I feel I am breaking up in health."[52] He was suffering from a severe pain in his chest, which may have been due to his practice, when on home missions in Mexico years previously, of beating his breast with a large stone when preaching. It is possible that he had thus caused a fracture of the *sternum*, which would have caused much pain, increasing as he grew older. He was also probably feeling the beginning of the heart failure that eventually caused his death.

Final Ordeal

There was, however, one final trial Fr. Junípero had to face before he went to his eternal reward. By the beginning of 1784, worrisome rumours were arriving from Lower California that the Franciscans were to be removed from Upper California and their missions entrusted to the Dominican friars. Junípero's response was amazing; one would have expected him to say that this was outrageous and unfair, but he did not. He wrote to Lasuén:

> The possibility of our being driven out of territories in which we were the first and only ones who announced the name of the true God, of Jesus Christ, and of His holy Gospel, of our being expelled from countries where we were the first to unfurl the Standard of the Cross—lands which count thousands of people baptized, some living, others dead—of other good Fathers in the near future coming here to take over . . .—all of this would furnish much ground for reflection. . . .
>
>   What shall be our reply? That it is the time to look within and amend my ways.[53]

The rumour had come because of a grandiose scheme dreamed up this time by the new bishop of the *Provincias Internas*, Bishop Reyes of Sonora, himself a Franciscan. He suggested to Madrid that they reduce the numbers of friars, which would mean a saving on expenditure. The College of San Fernando in Mexico City was totally opposed to the project, which is why Bishop Reyes turned to the Dominicans in Lower California and asked them to take over from the Franciscans. Fortunately, Count de Gálvez, as Minister of State in Madrid, was able to block the scheme and to see that it was later abandoned; but it had elicited from Fr. Serra an impressive

PAGES 112–113   *Fr. Serra's room at Mission San Carlos Borromeo*

expression of his detachment and of his total acceptance of the will of God. He wrote to the president of San Fernando:

> God's will be done.
>
> If those who come to eject us do better than we have done, we have no reason to complain. It is our duty to wish for progress in the work of God. And yet it would seem they would be better advised to exercise their fervor among some other set of savages, and not take from us. But God's ways are beyond our knowing.
>
> If the Lord wishes it so, or allows it to happen in this way—there is no more to say.[54]

Junípero's Death

In August 1784 Fr. Junípero, who had given several previous warnings about his health, felt that his end was near and asked Fr. Francisco Palóu to come at once to Mission Carmel. Palóu found him very weak but was surprised at the strength of his voice when it came to singing in church. One of the soldiers said to him: "[T]here is no basis for hope: he is ill. This saintly priest is always well when it comes to praying and singing, but he is nearly finished." [55] And so it proved to be. Fr. Serra's chest was badly congested; he passed the night kneeling on the floor with his breast against the board of his bed because that position gave him some relief—a detail, recorded by Palóu, which would confirm that he had increasing cardiac failure. On 27 August he asked for Viaticum (Holy Communion received at the hour of death), but he wanted it to be given in the church, with all solemnity, and not in his cell, as Palóu proposed. Junípero said that if he could go to the Lord there was no reason why the Lord should come to him. He walked the hundred yards to the church accompanied by the commander of the garrison and some of the soldiers. The word had spread among the natives, who all came up, too, and showed their affection for him at this hour when they felt he was going to be taken from them.

His last Communion was given with unusual solemnity; there was incense and the singing of the *Tantum Ergo*, which Junípero

Painting of Junípero Serra, which hangs in the Consistorial Hall of the
Ayuntamiento (City Hall) of Palma, Majorca, painted by Fray
Caymari c.1790. The painting depicts Junípero Serra as an old man at
the hour of his death. Fr. Palóu (on the right) is sprinkling the room
with holy water. One of the Spanish officers is on the left.

intoned in a loud voice as though he were in full health. He was always anxious to make an impression on his convert natives through the ceremonies of the Church, and on this occasion he wanted to instruct them, too, through his example. He remained kneeling at the side of the altar in deep recollection, and when he got up and slowly returned to his little room, the whole assembly accompanied him, and many of the people were crying because they knew that their Padre was going to leave them.

"Read me the Commendation for a Departing Soul, and say it aloud so I can hear it."

That night he felt worse and received the anointing with the Oil of the Sick. He was very uncomfortable again and sat on the floor, leaning on the breast of some of his convert natives. They spent the whole night in his cell. Being unable to lie flat in bed would indicate progressive cardiac failure, which ultimately was to lead to his death by coronary thrombosis. The next day, 28 August, he seemed better and sat on a little rush-bottomed chair, leaning against the bed. He was able to stand to greet some Spanish officers and listen to them talking about their voyage to Peru; then he gave instructions about where he wanted to be buried. Sometime afterwards he asked Fr. Palóu to sprinkle the room with holy water and said: "Great fear has come upon me; I have a great fear. Read me the Commendation for a Departing Soul, and say it aloud so I can hear it." [56] Then Palóu read the magnificent text of the *Commendatio animae* from the Roman Ritual, beginning with the words *"Proficiscere anima christiana de hoc mundo"*, Go forth, Christian soul, from this world. Junípero made all the responses with that strong voice of his, as though he were well. Kneeling around him were the Spanish officers, the two Franciscans and many of the soldiers and natives. When the long prayer was finished, Fr. Junípero cried out, "Thanks be to God, thanks be to God, all fear has now left me. Thanks be to God, I have no more fear, and so let us go outside." [57]

So they went to the next room, where Junípero sat on a chair and said some of the hours of the Divine Office. As it was one o'clock in the afternoon, Fr. Palóu persuaded him to take a cup of broth, after which Junípero said, "Now let us go to rest", and walked back to his cell, where he lay down on his bed with the cross on his breast, held in his arms. Fr. Palóu left him to go and look after dinner for the officers; then, as he tells us, "after a short time I returned and approached his bed to see if he was sleeping. I found him just as we had left him a little before, but now asleep in the Lord, without having given any sign or trace of agony, his body showing no other sign of death than the cessation of breathing; on the contrary, he seemed to be sleeping." [58] The lack of any evidence of disturbance or distress would indicate that the moment of death was sudden, probably caused by acute left ventricular failure.

As soon as the bells began to toll, crowds of natives flocked to the mission; many were in tears as they tried to get a glimpse of their Father Junípero for the last time. In fact, it was impossible to place his body in the coffin until his cell had been cleared of the crowd. When it was readmitted, hundreds filed past the open coffin. Palóu described how "[t]hey were praying to him and touching rosaries and medals to his venerable hands and face, openly calling him 'Holy Father,' 'Blessed Father,' and other names dictated by the love they bore him, and by the heroic virtues which they had witnessed in him during life." [59] When it became dark, the body was taken in procession to the church. There was such a crowd that Fr. Palóu agreed to leave the church open, so that they could sing the Rosary and pray all night, but he put a watch of two soldiers near the body.

On the day after his death, Junípero was buried in the Church at Mission San Carlos Borromeo de Carmelo, near Monterey. The Spaniards tried to give him as grand a funeral as possible, conscious as they were of what California owed to this one man who had been *padre presidente* for fifteen years. In the morning four priests were present at the Requiem Mass. The cannon of the supply ship anchored in the bay fired every half hour, and the guns of the *presidio* responded. At four in the afternoon, when the greatest heat was past, Junípero's coffin was taken in procession round the square of the mission. Officers from the army and the navy took it in turns to carry it and four stations were made, at each of which an antiphon was sung. Then the coffin was brought back to the church and buried within the altar rails, on the Gospel side of the sanctuary. Perhaps more impressive was the tribute from the natives, whom Junípero loved so much and served so well. Their crying and wailing almost drowned the singing of the Office for the Dead. Palóu is surely right in commenting: "The ceremony was concluded with a sung response, but the tears, sighs and cries of those assisting drowned out the voices of the chanters. The sons were lamenting the death of their father who, having left his own aging parents in his homeland, had come to this distant place for the sole purpose of making them his spiritual children and children of God through holy Baptism." [60] This was Junípero Serra's finest epitaph.

POSTSCRIPT

POSTSCRIPT

The End of the Missions

After the death of Fr. Junípero Serra, the Indian missions in California continued to develop, and new missions were founded up to 1823, bringing the total number to twenty-one. The whole system, however, collapsed ten years later. One factor in its demise was the effect of European-carried diseases on a native population devoid of immunities. As had happened in Mexico, European diseases affected the population of California immediately after the arrival of the Spaniards; epidemics became chronic and caused heavy loss of life, both among the natives who remained in their villages and among those who lived in the missions. Tuberculosis and syphilis, both of which had been present in America even before the arrival of Christopher Columbus, were widespread in California, venereal diseases being responsible probably for the low fertility rate of the missions. In addition, the communal life would have encouraged contagion, as did, no doubt, the prevalent conditions of sanitation and waste disposal.[1]

The other causes of collapse were political. In 1833 the government of Mexico decreed the secularisation of the Californian missions. Mexico had declared itself independent of Spain in 1821, so that secularisation in California was not carried out by royal officials from Madrid. Many greedy eyes were fixed on mission lands, some of the Mexican officials being the most eager to create farms and ranches for themselves and their relatives. In the Spanish colonial empire, secularisation had meant the handing over of the mission as a parish to a secular (that is, diocesan) priest and the setting up of a town administration with *alcaldes* and *regidores*, as Governor de Neve had wanted to do in 1779. Fr. Serra considered then that such a handover was premature, but when it did come, it led to the rapid eviction of the Californian natives. Although the land was handed over to them in theory, they were incapable of using it properly and were often unaware of the significance of the transaction; they were soon cheated out of their property; sometimes they gambled their rights away; in other cases speculators bought their land for a fraction of its real value. By the 1830s the civil administration did not have the interests of the Californian natives at heart, so that no native *pueblos* replaced the flourishing missions that the Franciscans had worked so hard to establish. In 1848 the Gold Rush began, and tens of thousands of Americans from the eastern states trekked west in search of fortune. For a short time, a part of California declared itself independent of Mexico and hoisted a flag with a bear and a star, inscribed *Californian Republic*, but the new republic did not last long. (California became a part of the United States in 1850, and the Bear Flag is now the flag of the State of California.) Although most of the new arrivals did not make a fortune from gold digging, they did settle in California, and they wanted land. The natives were either wiped out or driven off their ancestral territories. Survivors were herded into reservations on the poorest lands of the new state.

Missionary Methods

If the work of civilisation that Fr. Junípero and his friars had tried to achieve seemed to have led to nothing, their missionary method was also soon discredited. It had been possible only because of the high degree of integration of the Church into the Spanish colonial system, institutionalised under the name of the *patronato real*. Most missionaries in the history of the Church had worked under very different conditions. In the nineteenth century, the European missions to Africa did not try to create separate cultural and economic entities under the control of missionaries. Priests and sisters went to live in the midst of tribal communities and to preach the gospel from there. However, their presence was often guaranteed by colonial powers, and the creation of a local church was still envisaged on a European model.

> *. . . there are many elements in native cultures that are the result of divine truth and justice . . .*

After the Second World War, a group of French theologians started to advocate the recognition of values in other religions and a new understanding of mission that would take these values into account. This is the model that was adopted by the Second Vatican Council (1962–1965). The Council stated that there are many elements in native cultures that are the result of divine truth and justice, so that Christian life needs to be adapted to the genius and character of a culture and to its particular traditions. The Council speaks of restoring to Christ "those elements of truth and grace which are found among peoples, and which are, as it were, a secret presence of God",[2] so "whatever goodness is found in the minds and hearts of men, or in the particular customs and cultures of peoples, far from being lost is purified, raised to a higher level and reaches its perfection." [3]

Already at the time of the Council but mainly afterwards, German and Dutch theologians were developing a theology of non-Christian religions that recognised not only the existence of values in other religions but also their contribution to salvation. The Catholic Church has always taught that the grace of God is not limited to the visible Church; since the Council it has become clearer that grace can include some of the customs and rites of other faiths.[4] Mission has to be seen therefore as an encounter in which

both sides are changed and enriched. Such insights have gradually
led writers on mission to emphasise the importance of the community that is evangelised, because it is the local community that
integrates, in the light of the universal Christian tradition, its understanding of the gospel and its understanding of its own culture and
religion.

So we have to ask: Since the Spanish culture that Fr. Serra tried to
create among the natives of California has almost vanished, and
since his missionary methods have long been abandoned, where
exactly are his achievements to be sought? To answer that question,
it must be remembered that saints are not necessarily social reformers, nor are they always ahead of their times. As we have seen, Junípero's teaching when he was an academic was not innovative and
showed no sign of engaging with the problems of contemporary
philosophy and theology. As regards his struggle with administrators
imbued with the ideas of the Enlightenment, it would be wrong to
give the impression that eighteenth-century Enlightenment was entirely misguided. It had a role to play in purifying established
churches and in making clear the distinction between Church and
State, a distinction that often freed the Church for her development
in the nineteenth century. The situation that exists today in certain
Islamic countries because of the apparently inextricable bond between religion and the State illustrates some of the beneficial effects
of the European Enlightenment that these societies have never
experienced.

Holiness

The main reason Junípero Serra is relevant today is that he achieved
holiness. A French novelist, Georges Bernanos (1888–1948), once
wrote: "Holiness is the sole adventure, the sole reality which will
remain." And another French writer, Léon Bloy (1846–1917), said:

Native American Sculpture of Saint Benedict, Mission San Carlos Borromeo

"There is only one sadness, the sadness of not being a saint." If holiness is so important, then the Church has to be able to point to holiness as something that really does occur in every age and among human beings who share the limitations of which we are all conscious. The Church cannot merely acknowledge, as we all do, that there are some who are outstanding because of the combination of will-power, a happy temperament and a natural nobility of character. It must be able to point to lives, and often quite ordinary lives, that have been transformed by the inner presence and activity of the Holy Spirit.

Central to the Christian ideal of holiness is the call to become like Christ, especially in his desire to follow the will of his Father. The notion of calling is essential to that ideal, because it involves overcoming our self-centredness so as to follow Christ in poverty. The presence of the Holy Spirit, dwelling in the heart of a Christian, is the cause of holiness, because it is attributed, first, to the action of God in us, eliciting the response that characterises each individual. The gifts of the Spirit consecrate the personality and enrich it, so there is no dull uniformity in the calendar of the Church's saints. But in every case, the Spirit opens the individual to the community that is the Church, so that in the Christian tradition holiness is an exercise in community. It urges us to serve our brothers and sisters, to show them that same love we have received from God. It is nourished by the teaching of Jesus Christ as proclaimed by the Church, and by the sacraments of Christ as given in his community.

In 1948 the Diocese of Monterey began the formal examination of the life of Fr Junípero Serra to see whether it conformed to this ideal of holiness. The process involved an examination of his writings, his behaviour and all aspects of his life, in so far as they could be discovered from the historical evidence available. The question that had to be answered was: "Is it possible to infer from this evidence that Junípero Serra had that inner union with God, that following of Jesus Christ and those gifts of the Spirit that are the signs of holiness?" A further question was: "Has God indicated the supernatural holiness of his servant by working a miracle in answer to the prayers offered to him through the intercession of Fr. Junípero?"

As the careful process of examination progressed, adverse criticism of Spanish missionary methods and of Fr. Serra began to surface in America. It was part of a general reassessment of the colonial period and often an expression of the guilt American society feels about the ways in which native cultures have been treated. In this study, I have drawn attention to the shortcomings of Spanish missionary method, to its paternalism and to its attempts to make the natives into Spaniards. I have also underlined its good aspects, above all its respect for the right of California natives to their land, a right that was often ignored in areas of Anglo-Saxon settlement.

Genocide?

However, some criticism of the Franciscan missions in California is unwarranted; for instance, they have been compared to Nazi concentration camps because of the high rate of mortality, and the words "genocide" and "holocaust" have been applied to them. To make such a comparison is to ignore two facts: first, that Fr. Junípero allowed natives to join the missions only of their own free will; second, that the high mortality rate was not confined to the missions.

Fr. Junípero himself sought to establish the reasons why the missions were proving attractive to the natives, and he did so in a way that showed that new arrivals were coming in an unpredictable way. He wrote in 1774 to Viceroy Bucareli:

> From rancherias very far distant, and lost in the folds of the mountains, they arrive every day . . . they tell us frankly how delighted they would be if they had Fathers in their country. They see the Church and how attractive it looks; they see the cornfields which appear wonderful in their eyes; they see the throngs of children and

all the rest of the people, how they are all clothed, and sing and eat in plenty, even though they have to work. All this, together with the working of our Lord in their souls, who doubts that this wins their heart?[5]

High mortality because of diseases introduced by Europeans was a tragic accompaniment of the colonial period in both North and South America. Such mortality was not restricted to mission-type settlements; as has been said, it was widespread, wherever European and native populations came into contact. Although the concentration of population in the missions may have contributed to the spread of disease, it did not cause it, nor did it cause the epidemics that regularly decimated the native population. It is ironic that the mission system in California ended just at the time when immunities may have been developing in the native Californians, immunities that might have caused an upturn in the population, as had happened earlier in Mexico. Sherburne Friend Cook (1896–1974) carried out careful research on the conditions of life in the missions, and his conclusion on mortality rate was that "the worst period [of the death rate] was over before the missions closed, and it is perfectly possible, although not certain, that, had not secularisation and disruption occurred, the death rate might have fallen much lower."[6]

Even more surprising than these criticisms have been the allegations of cruelty levelled against Junípero Serra personally. Thus Ward Churchill, writing in 1997, calls Serra "a man whose personal brutality was noteworthy. . . . He appears to have delighted in the direct torture of victims, had to be restrained from hanging Indians in lots, à la Columbus, and is quoted as ascertaining that 'the entire race' of Indians 'should be put to the knife'."[7] Anyone who has read the pages of my study of Serra will know that such a description is radically different from the one that emerges from the contemporary evidence of Serra's own letters and Palóu's biography. Indeed, anyone who knows something of the Spanish colonial period will know that friars could never have hanged natives, either individually or in lots, since capital punishment was the exclusive prerogative of the civil authorities. How then could such a travesty of the truth be popularised in present-day California?

Professor Churchill gives a false reference for his astounding statements;[8] in fact, he is following David E. Stannard, whose study *American Holocaust*, described as "a work of impassioned scholarship" on the cover of the paperback edition, was published in 1992.[9] Professor Stannard refers to Palóu's *Noticias de la Nueva California*, in the English translation by H. E. Bolton, published in 1966.[10] One is astounded on reading the passage in question to find that it does not refer to Serra at all. It describes an incident that occurred in Lower California in 1768 and that involved "the visitor", that is, Count de Gálvez, who lost his temper with the Guianos Indians when they stole his dinner and his equipment: "His Lordship was so angered by all this that it was necessary for the fathers . . . to restrain him in order to prevent him from hanging some of them. . . . He shouted that such a race of people deserved to be put to the knife, so that they might not corrupt others." The text, far from giving evidence of the cruelty of the Franciscans, shows them begging for mercy for the natives from the civil authorities, a role that was frequently adopted by Fr. Serra himself, as has been noted in the account of his life. Yet on such a misreading of history is Fr. Junípero accused of "personal brutality".[11] Impassioned Professor Stannard's reading of history may be, but such misuse of his sources in this case can hardly be described as scholarly.

It is true that Fr. Junípero and the eighteenth-century Franciscans did not have the sensibility of twentieth-century Americans. They accepted a colonial society whose shortcomings are very clear today, just as the shortcomings of today's society will be clearer, no doubt, to future generations than they are to us. But within those limitations, Fr. Junípero gave his life completely to the missionary ideal as it was understood by the Church in the eighteenth century. The veneration in which he was held by the natives of California and the love they had for the one who was their father in God are the vindication of his work.

Miracles

Apart from the historical study of a candidate for sainthood and his or her historical context, the evidence of miracles is part of the process of canonisation. This may seem strange to the people of today, but it stems from the biblical understanding of miracles as signs of the saving power of God. In the New Testament the miracles of Jesus are signs of his ultimate victory over sin and death. Miracles of healing especially indicate that the power of God is at work, restoring that wholeness of body and spirit that had been destroyed by original sin. Jesus has come to take away sin; his taking away of disease is a sign of the redemption, of which his Resurrection is the complete manifestation. By miracles of healing, which God may grant in response to prayers addressed to his saints, he indicates that they have reached the fullness of the Kingdom. Reports of miracles are therefore examined as part of the process of canonisation, since they can be an indication that the candidate for sainthood has in fact reached that fullness of redemption which is the state of the blessed in heaven.

Stories of miracles connected with Fr. Junípero were, in fact, handed down among the native families of Monterey and Carmel. These stories were recounted by witnesses who were examined by the tribunal of the Diocese of Monterey in 1949. They were stories of the presence of Fr. Junípero at the bedside of the dying in a way that cannot be naturally explained. For instance, one of them recounts that Fr. Junípero had been on the way to a sick person and had sat down at the roadside because of his age and his sore leg and had fallen into deep prayer. Then he said to his companions, "Let us return to the mission, for all is taken care of"; meanwhile, the sick persons had actually received the sacraments from him. Another story tells of a man who rode over from Monterey to Mission Carmel to ask Fr. Serra to come to his wife, who was very ill, and to give her the last sacraments. The man had brought another horse so that the padre could ride back with him, but Junípero Serra refused to ride and said that he would be at the side of his wife by the time the man got back, which he was. These stories, which had a long history of oral transmission and were no doubt influenced by folk-lore, could not be corroborated at the time of the process.

The report that was submitted to the Congregation for the Causes of Saints in Rome concerned a cure that had happened to Sister Mary Boniface Dyrda, O.S.F., in 1960. She was teaching at Todd's Mill, Illinois, in October 1959, when she suddenly suffered from rash, fever, weakness and swelling all over her body. One day she found herself unable to walk back from church. She was hospitalised at Centralia, Illinois, then at De Paul Hospital, North St. Louis, but doctors could not determine the cause of her illness. She was actually suffering from *Systemic Lupus Erythematosus*, a multisystem connective tissue disease, in this case presenting origi-nally as *Lupus Erythematosus*, a chronic skin condition. The cause of S.L.E. remains obscure, but current theory is that it is a multifacto-rial disorder with profound disturbance of immune regulation. In the case of Sister Boniface Dyrda, X-rays revealed that she had an enlarged spleen, which was removed, and this would have made her even more susceptible to infection, a common cause of morbidity. By spring 1960 she had suffered catastrophic loss of weight; she received the Last Rites on Palm Sunday and was not expected to live for more than twenty-four hours.

Meanwhile, the Franciscan chaplain to the sisters had started a novena to Fr. Junípero Serra to pray for Sister Boniface Dyrda's re-covery. Instead of death, a rapid improvement in her condition oc-curred, accompanied by the complete and permanent disappearance of the symptoms of the disease. The doctors who examined the case could only record that there was no medical explanation for the cure. The Congregation for the Causes of Saints at Rome examined the evidence of her condition, the testimony of witnesses and the medical records. As a result of that examination, Pope John Paul II declared on 11 December 1987 that a miraculous cure had occurred. He proceeded to proclaim the beatification of Fr. Junípero Serra in St. Peter's Square on 25 September 1988, declaring that his feast day would be celebrated annually on 28 August.

At the centre of holiness is love, love for the incarnate God in whom the fullness of the Godhead has been revealed, love for our fellow men and women. Holiness is ultimately a communion and a resting in the beloved. This experience of communion is illustrated in a touching way by the practise of Fr. Junípero described by Fr. Francisco Palóu, his fellow disciple and friend. He tells us about Junípero's practice of sleeping with the cross in his arms, and how he did this on the day of his death:

> Along the road he used to do the same thing. He would stretch the blanket and a pillow on the ground, and he would lie down on these to get his necessary rest. He always slept with a crucifix upon his breast, in the embrace of his hands. It was about a foot in length. He had carried it with him from the time he was in the novitiate at the college, nor did he ever fail to have it with him. On all his journeys he carried it with him, together with the blanket and pillow. At his mission, and whenever he stopped, as soon as he got up from bed he placed the crucifix upon the pillow. Thus he had it . . . on the day when he was to deliver his soul to his Creator.[12]

CREDITS

REFERENCES AND NOTES

MAJORCA

1. Four Catholic priests are commemorated in the Hall of Fame of the Capitol. In addition to Junípero Serra, they are Jacques Marquette, S.J. (Louisiana), Eusebio Kino, S.J. (Arizona), and Blessed Damian de Veuster (Hawaii).

2. Letter to Fr. Francesch Serra, 20 August 1749, *Writings of Junípero Serra*, ed. Antonine Tibesar, O.F.M. (Washington, D.C.: Academy of American Franciscan History, 1955–1966), 1:5.

3. Francisco Palóu, *Palóu's Life of Fray Junípero Serra*, translated and annotated by Maynard J. Geiger, O.F.M. (Washington, D.C.: Academy of American Franciscan History, 1955), 5. The original, *Relación histórica de la vida y apostolicas tareas del venerable padre Fray Junípero Serra*, was published in Mexico City in 1787.

4. Biblioteca Publica de Palma de Mallorca, Ms. no. 1085, fol. 132.

5. Letter to Fr. Francesch Serra, 20 August 1749, in Tibesar, *Writings*, 1:3.

6. Palóu, *Life*, 13.

7. Letter to Fr. Francesch Serra, 14 December 1749, in Tibesar, *Writings*, 1:11.

MEXICO

1. Francisco Palóu, *Palóu's Life of Fray Junípero Serra*, translated and annotated by Maynard J. Geiger, O.F.M. (Washington, D.C.: Academy of American Franciscan History, 1955), 19–20.

2. Ibid., 45–46.

3. Ibid., 41–42.

CALIFORNIA

1. "E cil d'Affrike et cil de Califerne", *Chanson de Roland*, canto 239, line 2924.

2. On the whole question of the impact on health and morbidity of the arrival of Europeans in America, see *Disease and Demography in the Americas*, ed. John W. Verano and Douglas H. Ubelaker (Washington, D.C.: Smithsonian Institution Press, 1992), containing the contributions to the symposium "Disease and Demography in the Americas: Changing Patterns before and after 1492" held in November 1989.

3. "The paleopathology chapters here, together with many others in the anthropological literature, clearly document the presence of malnutrition, anaemia, and a variety of tuberculoid, trepanematoid [venereal disease], and other infections as well as trauma and degenerative conditions. This body of data is now so well established that the concept of a pristine, disease-free pre-Columbian New World environment is no longer credible": Arthur C. Aufderheide, "Summary on Disease before and after Contact", in ibid., 165.

4. Bernard E. Bobb, *The Viceregency of Antonio Maria Bucareli in New Spain 1771–1779* (Austin: University of Texas Press, 1962), 25.

5. Letter to Fr. Francisco Palóu, 10 February 1770, *Writings of Junípero Serra*, edited by Antonine Tibesar, O.F.M. (Washington, D.C.: Academy of American Franciscan History, 1955–1966), 1:161.

6. Expedition Journal, 2 June 1769, ibid., 1:83.

7. Ibid., 15 May 1769, 1:63.

8. Ibid., 21 May 1769, 1:67.

9. Ibid.

10. Ibid., 1 July 1769, 1:121.

11. "These enormous mountains are almost entirely of pure soil": ibid., 2 June 1769, 1:83.

12. Letter to Viceroy de Croix, 18 June 1771, ibid., 1:209.

13. Letter to Fr. Juan Andrés, 3 July 1769, ibid., 1:139.

14. Report on the Missions, 1 July 1784, ibid., 4:273.

15. Letter to Viceroy Bucareli, 21 May 1773, ibid., 1:359.

16. Letter to Fr. Juan Sancho, 29 October 1783, ibid., 4:203.

17. Report on the Missions, 1 July 1784, ibid., 4:257.

18. Letter to Fr. Juan Andrés, 12 June 1770, ibid., 1:173.

19. "The lack of wine for Mass is becoming unbearable. That we remain . . . without chocolate or snuff is regrettable": letter to Fr. Fermín Francisco Lasuén, 8 December 1781, ibid., 4:101.

20. "[N]ow that we have plenty of wax, which was very scarce before, this other trouble [the shortage of wine] crops up": letter to Fr. Francisco Palóu, 21 June 1771, ibid., 1:243.

21. Letter to Fr. Miguel de Petra, 4 August 1773, ibid., 1:389.

22. Ibid., 1:391.

23. Letter to Fr. Francisco Palóu, 21 June 1771, ibid., 1:241.

24. Letter to Fr. Franciso Pangua, 6 June 1777, ibid., 3:159.

25. Letter to Viceroy Bucareli, 13 March 1773, ibid., 1:307.

26. Ibid., 1:327.

27. Letter to Fr. Francisco Pangua, 14 June 1774, ibid., 2:71.

28. Letter to Viceroy Bucareli, 29 October 1775, ibid., 2:377.

29. Maynard Geiger, *The Life and Times of Fray Junípero Serra O.F.M.; or, The Man Who Never Turned Back* (Washington, D.C.: Academy of American Franciscan History, 1959), 2:342.

30. Letter to Viceroy Bucareli, 24 August 1774, in Tibesar, *Writings*, 2:139.

31. Letter to Governor Rivera, 24 July 1775, ibid., 2:285.

32. Francisco Palóu, *Palóu's Life of Fray Junípero Serra*, translated and annotated by Maynard J. Geiger, O.F.M. (Washington, D.C.: Academy of American Franciscan History, 1955), 167.

33. Letter to Viceroy Bucareli, 15 December 1775, in Tibesar, *Writings*, 2:407.

34. Letter to Viceroy Bucareli, 8 March 1773, *Correspondence*, vol. 5 of *Anza's California Expeditions*, translated and edited by Herbert Eugene Bolton (Berkeley, California: University of California Press, 1930), 69, 73.

35. 28 March 1776, *Font's Complete Diary of the Second Anza Expedition*, vol. 4 of ibid., 341.

36. Letter to Viceroy Bucareli, 13 March 1773, in Tibesar, *Writings*, 1:311.

37. Letter to Secretary de Peramas, 14 June 1774, ibid., 2:67.

38. Letter to Commander General de Croix, 22 August 1778, ibid., 3:253, 255.

39. Letter to Fr. Fermín Francisco Lasuén, 29 March 1779, ibid., 3:295.

40. Letter to Governor de Neve, 7 January 1780, ibid., 3:415.

41. Letter to Fr. Francisco Palóu, 18 August 1772, ibid., 1:269.

42. Letter to Fr. Francisco Pangua, 7 October 1776, ibid., 3:67.

43. Letter to Fr. Juan Sancho, 27 October 1783, ibid., 4:195.

44. Letter to Fr. Juan Figuer, 30 March 1779, ibid., 3:303.

45. Ibid., 305.

46. Ibid., 307.

47. Letter to Viceroy Bucareli, 1 March 1777, ibid., 3:113–15.

48. Palóu, *Life*, 273.

49. Letter to Fr. Francisco Pangua, 8 December 1782, in Tibesar, *Writings*, 4:169.

50. Letter to Fr. Rafael Verger, 19 August 1778, ibid., 3:233.

51. Letter to Fr. Juan Sancho, Feast of the Sacred Heart (18 June) 1784, ibid., 4:239.

52. Letter to Fr. Juan Sancho, 27 October 1783, ibid., 4:193.

53. Letter to Fr. Fermín Francisco Lasuén, 17 April 1784, ibid., 4:229–31.

54. Letter to Fr. Juan Sancho, 18 June 1784, ibid., 4:243.

55. Palóu, *Life*, 243.

56. Ibid., 247.

57. Ibid.

58. Ibid., 248.

59. Ibid., 249.

60. Ibid., 252.

POSTSCRIPT

1. Cf. Philip L. Walker and John R. Johnson, "Effects of Contact on the Chumash Indians", in *Disease and Demography in the Americas*, ed. John W.

Verano and Douglas H. Ubelaker (Washington, D.C.: Smithsonian Institution Press, 1992), 127–39.

2. Decree on the Church's Missionary Activity, *Ad Gentes Divinitus* (7 December 1965), no. 9.

3. Ibid.

4. Dogmatic Constitution on the Church, *Lumen Gentium* (21 November 1964), no. 17.

5. Letter to Viceroy Bucareli, 24 August 1774, *Writings of Junípero Serra*, ed. Antonine Tibesar, O.F.M. (Washington, D.C.: Academy of American Franciscan History, 1955–1966), 2:141.

6. S. F. Cook, *Population Trends among the Californian Mission Indians*, Ibero-Americana, no. 17 (Berkeley: University of California Press, 1940), 25.

7. Ward Churchill, *A Little Matter of Genocide: Holocaust and Denial in the Americas, 1492 to the Present* (San Francisco: City Light Books, 1997), 143.

8. Ward Churchill refers to W. James' translation of *Palóu's Life of Fray Junípero Serra*, 86-87, which contains nothing to support his allegation. Only the page number of his reference is correct, and it refers to a different work by Palóu, quoted by David E. Stannard. See n. 9 below.

9. David E. Stannard, *American Holocaust: Columbus and the Conquest of the New World* (New York: Oxford University Press, 1992).

10. *Historical Memoirs of New California, by Fray Francisco Palóu, O.F.M.,* translated into English from the manuscript in the archives of Mexico, ed. Herbert Eugene Bolton (New York: Russell and Russell, 1966), 1:86–87.

11. Churchill, *Genocide*, 143.

12. Francisco Palóu, *Palóu's Life of Fray Junípero Serra*, translated and annotated by Maynard J. Geiger, O.F.M. (Washington, D.C.: Academy of American Franciscan History, 1955), 246.

INDEX